KT-158-573

ATTACHMENT AND HUMAN SURVIVAL

Edited by

Marci Green

and

Marc Scholes

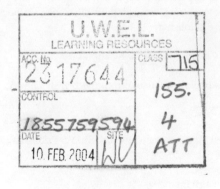

U.W.E.L.
LEARNING RESOURCES
ACC. No. 2317644
CONTROL 1855759594
DATE 10. FEB. 2004   SITE WU
CLASS 715
155.
4
ATT

KARNAC

LONDON   NEW YORK

WITHDRAWN

Published in 2004 by
H. Karnac (Books) Ltd.
6 Pembroke Buildings, London NW10 6RE

Copyright © 2004 Arrangement and Introduction, Marci Green and Marc Scholes
Chapters copyright © 2004 to individual contributors

The contributors assert the moral right to be identified as the authors
of this work.

All rights reserved. No part of this publication may be reproduced, stored in
a retrieval system, or transmitted, in any form or by any means, electronic,
mechanical, photocopying, recording, or otherwise, without the prior written
permission of the publisher.

British Library Cataloguing in Publication Data

A C.I.P. for this book is available from the British Library

ISBN 1 85575 959 4

Edited, designed, and produced by The Studio Publishing Services Ltd,
Exeter EX4 8JN

Printed in Great Britain

10 9 8 7 6 5 4 3 2 1

www.karnacbooks.com

CONTENTS

ACKNOWLEDGMENTS

The idea for this book emerged in the early Spring of 2002, and in less than two years it has come to fruition. We have numerous people to thank for making this possible. Certainly, we are indebted to the contributors who embraced the principles of the project and gave their time and effort so generously despite heavy commitments to teaching, clinical practice and publishing. We would also like to thank Sir Richard Bowlby and Susan Akehurst for their participation during early exploratory discussions. Joan Woodward, one of our contributors, has also advised on the direction and development of the book. We are grateful for her steady presence.

Colleagues at the University of Wolverhampton have been tremendously helpful. In particular, we are indebted to Andy Cameron in Sociology for his observations and suggestions on the material; to Lesley Tennick for helping us organise interview work in the United States; to Yolanda Granja-Rubio for her hard administrative labours and good humour in the preparation of the manuscript and to Drs Pauline Anderson (Head of Sociology) and A. J. Cooper (Head of Social Sciences) for their faith in and support of the project since its inception. We would also like to thank Justine

Sawkins (University of Central England) and Richard Sealey; they saw in this book an idea of journey and redemption, and helped us express this in the cover design.

Marci Green
Marc Scholes
Autumn 2003

CONTRIBUTORS

Felicity de Zulueta is a consultant psychiatrist in psychotherapy heading the Traumatic Stress Service at the Maudsley Hospital, London and an Honorary Senior Clinical Lecturer in Traumatic Studies at the Institute of Psychiatry. She studied medicine at Cambridge University and became a consultant psychotherapist in Charing Cross Hospital. Dr de Zulueta is a Group Analyst and a Systemic Family Therapist whose main interests lie in the study of attachment, psychological trauma, and bilingualism. She is author of *Pain to Violence: The Traumatic Roots of Destructiveness* (1993). She is also a founding member of the International Attachment Network.

Marci Green is a Senior Lecturer in Sociology at the University of Wolverhampton, specializing in political economy, the labour process, structures of inequality, and social theory. Her past publications have been on political economy, immigration, race-thinking, and national identity. Over the past five years, she has been devoting her time to Attachment Theory and Attachment Therapy, and is now exploring the implications of Attachment Theory for the fields of human rights and conflict resolution.

Peter Marris was associated with the Institute of Community Studies, London, for seventeen years, and then the Centre for Environmental Studies, before joining the Urban Planning Programme at the University of California, Los Angeles, from 1976 to 1991. He has taught at The University of California, Berkeley, MIT, Boston University, The University of Massachusetts, Boston, Brandeis University, Makerere University, and Yale, where he is presently a lecturer. Peter has undertaken research on housing and local economic development, community action and loss, in both Britain and the United States, and in East and West Africa. His books include *The Politics of Uncertainty: Attachment in Public and Private Life; Meaning and Action; Loss and Change;* and *Dilemmas of Social Reform* (with Martin Rein). A recent monograph, *Witnesses, Engineers and Storytellers, Using Research for Social Policy and Community Action,* reflects on his experience of research in the context of policy and social action.

Chris Purnell is a psychotherapist and a registered member of the Centre for Attachment-based Psychoanalytic Psychotherapy (CAPP). He is currently a psychotherapist and psychotherapy service manager with Wolverhampton City Primary Care Trust. Chris has an interest in and extensive experience of psychotherapeutic work with trauma and long-term illness, particularly HIV and AIDS, and has presented papers on this subject at local, national, and international level. He has also published in the *British Journal of Psychotherapy.*

Marc Scholes moved into academia about fourteen years ago as a researcher at the European Institute for the Media, following a career in media production. He has been at the University of Wolverhampton for twelve years now and is currently subject leader for Media, Communication and Cultural Studies. Previously, his publications have been in the field of media policy and regulation.

Daniel J. Siegel is an associate clinical professor of psychiatry at the UCLA Center for Culture, Brain, and Development. He is the founder and editor of the Norton Series on Interpersonal Neurobiology, and the author of *The Developing Mind: How Relationships* *and the Brain Interact to Shape Who We Are* and of *Parenting from the Inside Out: How a Deeper Self-Understanding Can Help You Raise Children Who Thrive.*

Jeremy Woodcock is the Director of Family Therapy training at the University of Bristol and is also in private practice as a psychotherapist. He worked for many years as a psychotherapist at the Medical Foundation for the Care of Victims of Torture and continues to take an active role in training in psychosocial work with refugees. He is particularly influenced by the insights of attachment theory and how they offer a bridge between systemic and psychoanalytic therapies, and the social–political world. His publications include a chapter in *Post Traumatic Stress Disorder in Children and Adolescents,* published by Whurr in 2000, and articles in *Context: The Newsletter of Family Therapy and Systemic Practice* (2000) and the *Journal of Family Therapy* (2001).

Joan Woodward is an Attachment-based psychotherapist, author and researcher. She started her professional life as a psychiatric social worker, and was a founder member of The Birmingham Women's counselling and Therapy Centre (UK). She now takes a particular interest in the psychological aspects of ageing. She is the author of *Understanding Ourselves* (Macmillan, 1988) and *The Lone Twin* (FAB) in 1998.

Introduction

Marci Green

"For some years now there has been proof that the devastating effects of the traumatization of children take their inevitable toll on society. This knowledge concerns every single one of us, and—if disseminated widely enough—should lead to fundamental changes in society, above all to a halt in the blind escalation of violence. ..."

(Miller, 2001, p. 281)

Miller's comment comes at the end of her book, *For Your Own Good*, a moving exploration of the causes and consequences of childhood suffering. One of the messages at the heart of her work is that the traumas of childhood are not just limited to a minority of the population; abuses arise from the everyday, ordinary, and routine beliefs and practices which shape the way children are brought up by their parents and valued by society. Her work is an appeal for adults to learn what children need, and be responsible for their care. It is also a plea to care-givers and policy-makers to understand that the experiences of personal suffering in one generation may yield social dysfunction and violence in the next.

John Bowlby, the originator of Attachment Theory, understood the intimate connection between our early life experiences, our emotional development, and our ability to relate with others. This connection resides in the quality of our earliest attachments; these are the unique relationships—between an infant and primary care-giver—through which a child's brain develops and emotional capacities emerge. The abilities of a human being subsequently to establish attachments rest profoundly on that person's early attachment experiences, whether they are "secure" or have "failed". Early secure attachments enable healthy mental and relational development, affording protection against the traumas of separation and loss. Failed attachments disrupt this development, limit one's relational capacities and lead to lifelong suffering.

Attachments are interpersonal and interactional, and rest on intimate communication. The quality of these attachments, however, is influenced by many things. Primary amongst these is the care-giver's ability to respond to an infant in sensitive and appropriate ways—an ability which, in turn, has been shaped by the adult care-giver's own early childhood attachment experiences. Furthermore, these interactions take place in the wider social settings of family, peers, communities, and institutional arrangements, settings that influence the emotional resources a care-giver can bring to the child. Supporting these resources are, for example, stability of domestic arrangements; security of income, food, and housing; and protection against the disruptions of violence and war.

Inseparable connections therefore exist amongst our attachment experiences, the resources of our communities, and the kinds of people we become. In turn, the kinds of people we become will determine the attachment experiences we are capable of giving to our children, our engagement with others in the public arenas of institutional life, and the kinds of societies we sustain. The truth of these connections, we believe, is beyond dispute, and for this reason we are convinced that knowledge of the conditions for secure attachments should be at the heart of our institutional, cultural, and political life. It should inform the ways that we parent, create social policy, shape the economy, and govern our domestic and international political relations. However, it is also our conviction that we live in societies that fail to comprehend and value human attachment as a condition for individual and species survival. It is for these reasons that this book has been written.

To understand the importance and character of attachments, we begin our discussion by exploring some of the key principles of Attachment Theory. These are summarized by Joan Woodward in Chapter One. She sets out, simply and clearly, the basic themes emerging from the work of Bowlby and others. Importantly, she reminds us that, in many respects, we already know how vital attachments are to life. In this chapter she helps us understand how and why that is the case.

One of the reasons why attachment experiences are so crucial to emotional development is that they influence brain development. In Chapter Two, Dan Siegel explores the ways in which intimate communications between infant and care-giver shape the neural pathways of the infant's brain and influence the child's eventual abilities to regulate his or her emotions and to respond to others in flexible and empathic ways. Significantly, Siegel also demonstrates that the brain is a social and adaptive organ, such that while early trauma may shape the developing mind in significant ways, later relationships may provide the healing experiences that can enable individuals to live healthful lives. The most powerful predictor of a child's security of attachment is actually the ways in which a parent has come to understand his or her own life experiences, not merely what those experiences actually were.

Given that our abilities as parents to make secure attachments with our children rest on an array of social as well as emotional resources, it useful to reflect on the cultural and institutional environments in which attachment relationships are formed. After all, how we order our relationships with children and others, will be shaped by the cultural and institutional settings in which we operate. In Chapter Three, Marci Green and Marc Scholes suggest that there may be real conflict between the conditions that are necessary for secure attachments, and the culture and organization of our key social institutions. They consider this conflict in relation to the institution of education.

In Chapter Four, Joan Woodward continues the theme of culture and attachments in her discussion of attachments, ageing and ageism. Attachments are essential, from the cradle to the grave, yet we live in societies that view older members of a population as "non-persons". Such ageist views deprive older people of the emotional sustenance they need to live well, and undervalue the rich resources that people of experience bring to their communities. Woodward's chapter also invites us to reflect more generally on the ways that all processes of social exclusion limit our understanding of attachment needs.

It is our position that the health of societies ultimately rests on the care we give to our children. Our ability to give this care, however, will be influenced by our material and emotional resources. These are unequally distributed. Peter Marris argues in Chapter Five, that the conditions of competitive capitalism that drive our global economies generate inequalities and may weaken the capacities of individuals and communities to sustain the health and welfare of their members. This situation derives, in part, from economic policies whose short-term strategies to encourage invest-ment may generate economic and social instability and uncertainty, states of being that influence our attachment systems.

Early experiences of unwilling separation and loss are central themes in Bowlby's work. However, the traumas that these generate are not limited to childhood and our capacity to cope with them partly depends on our early attachment relationships. In Chapter Six, Jeremy Woodcock explores the issues of trauma and attachment in the context of political torture and the violence of war. He helps us understand that, among other things, one of the objectives of torture is to deprive individuals and communities of the attach-ments on which psychological security is based. Furthermore, the devastation that such violence wreaks is not limited to individuals, since it can also destroy the psychological resources of communities over generations.

In Chapter Seven, Felicity de Zulueta continues the theme of personal suffering and public violence. She suggests that there is an intimate connection between failed attachments in childhood and later expressions of violent behaviour. Importantly, she argues that our attachment systems operate within the context of culture and society, so that societies that treat their members in unequal, injurious, and punitive ways help to legitimate and condone violence and facilitate the process by which one's personal pain is played out in public ways. She looks at this process in relation to domestic violence, community crime, and war.

Early attachment experiences structure our ability to feel safe within ourselves and to enter secure attachments throughout our lives. When those attachments "fail", the ways we cope with our internal insecurity may actually maintain the very pain and suffering we so hope to relieve. Thankfully, though, we are not condemned to live with attachment failures. In Chapter Eight, Chris Purnell explores the opportunities that attachment-based psychotherapy can provide to help individuals and families honour and make sense of their past, with a view to reclaiming their present and their future.

Chapter Nine invites readers to reflect on the experiences of, and recovery from, early failed attachments. This anonymous contribution is a personal account of a journey from pain to liberation and we are honoured that the author has offered to share her experience with us.

This book is intended for a wide, lay audience. It is our hope that it will encourage readers to understand that the ways we treat our children shape our quality of life, that the responsibility for emotional health and human development belongs to us all, and that attachments matter from the cradle to the grave.

CHAPTER ONE

Introduction to attachment theory

Joan Woodward

I hope that this introduction to Attachment Theory will help those to whom it is unfamiliar to realize that in some sense they have "known" about it ever since they can remember. I believe that this is because Attachment Theory is a theory of human development that makes sense to us all if we are able to examine our lives with honesty. We may be reluctant to apply it to ourselves, for all sorts of reasons, but it is a theory that we can readily understand and we can often quite easily see how it applies to other people that we know well.

Dr John Bowlby took over ten years to write his book *Attachment, Separation and Loss*, in which he first formulated Attachment Theory. He wrote it originally as three separate books, over the period of 1969 to 1980, though they are now put together as one. He defined Attachment Theory as: "A way of conceptualising ✗ the propensity of human beings to make strong affectional bonds to particular others". (Bowlby, 1979) He came to this conclusion after spending years observing the relationship between children and their mothers. He chose to study the maternal–child relationship because of its universality. It exists not only in all human cultures but also in the animal world. The detailed observations that Bowlby made led him to recognize that we humans, like some animals, have an *instinctive behaviour pattern* that leads us to make these strong affectional bonds to particular others. He saw that these bonds are quite different from the *generalized*, so-called "dependency needs" described by earlier psychoanalysts. (Bowlby thought that some analysts described these needs in disparaging ways.) Indeed, he believed that strong affectional bonds exist throughout our lives and are not something "babyish" to grow out of. Furthermore, these bonds are highly *particular* in that they are directed at a few individuals in a clear order of preference. Nearly everyone knows immediately who their closest attachment figure is. Babies know this even before they are able to articulate it. Most people can list three or four other attachment figures in descending order following their primary one without difficulty and then find that they do not differentiate much after that.

Another characteristic of our bonds to attachment figures that Bowlby recognized, is that they *endure*. That is to say, they are not easily abandoned; although they change as we get older, they persist and become supplemented by new bonds. Bowlby, unlike other psychoanalysts recognized that it is our affectional bonds to attachment figures that engage us in our most intense emotions. This occurs during their formation (we call that "falling in love"), in their maintenance (which we describe as "loving"), and in their loss (which we know as "grieving"). If the loss of these bonds is threatened, both anxiety and anger are aroused. Their actual loss gives rise to sorrow, but their renewal is a source of joy.

Bowlby claimed that there are two essential features of attachment figures. One is that they serve the *biological* function of securing protection for survival. The second is that they will meet a *psychological* need for security, which is vital for human development. In contrast to so many other animals, humans take a long time to develop. The more "civilized" and complicated the lives of humans become, the longer is the period of time for which they need protection through secure attachment. Bowlby recognized that for some people, as adults, important attachments included institutions or organizations to which they belonged, and he believed that often within these there were leaders or top figures that were of great importance.

Bowlby had a very different background from many of his

contemporaries in both medicine and psychoanalysis, because he was equally interested in ethology, which is the scientific study of animals. He was influenced by the work of other ethologists and saw how relevant their findings were to his understanding of human development. Lorenz, in his widely known study (Lorenz, 1935), showed how a newly hatched gosling followed a shoebox pulled along on a string to imitate a moving figure. The gosling's *instinctive behaviour* made it follow the shoebox as if it was its mother, as being closely attached to its mother is the overriding need of the baby gosling to secure its survival. This study into the bonding patterns in geese confirmed for Bowlby the role of attachment in the protection of the young.

The other ethological study that probably influenced Bowlby even more, was one undertaken by Harlow. His work with baby monkeys showed that their need for attachment to their mothers gave them a sense of security, and this need actually *took priority over their need for food*. Harlow created an experiment setting up two model mother monkeys. One was made of a wire frame with a bottle of milk at nipple level. The other was made of soft fur without any milk being available. The baby monkeys showed preference for the fur "mother", and attached themselves to her as if she was real (Harlow & Zimmerman, 1959). It was studies such as these, as well as those of human mothers and their babies, that led Bowlby slowly to formulate his Attachment Theory and to clarify the differences it held from the theoretical beliefs of previous psychoanalysts, particularly Freud and Klein.

To understand Attachment Theory it is necessary to appreciate the great struggle Dr Bowlby went through to get it recognized as a theory of human development. It deeply challenged the basic principles of classical psychoanalysis held in his day and led to some shameful hostilities towards him personally. For example, the Freudian School believed that we have one great instinctive drive that Freud named "libido" and that this drove us to find *physiological satisfactions* through the two main sources of food and sex. Freud believed that levels of anxiety arose when these primary needs were not satisfied. In Freud's view it is the mother who is the source, or "object", as it came to be described, who will meet, or fail to meet, these needs. Klein so markedly saw the mother in these terms that she formulated the idea of the "Good Breast" as

aby's needs (and that the baby "took in"), or the
t dissatisfied, and thus left the baby empty. Bowlby
these theories because, in his view, both Freud and
ee that the attachment between an infant and its
mother is a *psychological bond* and not one based on an instinctive
drive for feeding or infantile sexuality. Bowlby thought that the
views of Freud and Klein reduced the bond to mere "cupboard
love". He went so far as to say that he believed the young child's
hunger for his mother's love and presence is as great as his hunger
for food.

Bowlby's belief may seem extreme, but it has been borne out by
studies such as the one that Spitz made of how small children
behaved when separated from their mothers. He studied and
compared two groups of young children. One group got a good
deal of mothering as they were in residential care with their
mothers. The other group were described as "foundling" children
who had no contact with their mothers. For this second group there
was only one nurse, who served as an "attachment figure" for about
nine children. The film he made showed the latter group of children
in great distress, rocking themselves for hours on end, and a high
proportion of them died from infections (Spitz, 1945). Bowlby never
denied the essential need for food and sex, but he saw these as
instinctive behaviours among others and did not hold the "primary
motivational system" of attachment.

Another, and vital, way in which Bowlby's work differed from
that of his predecessors was that he observed and listened to
people's *actual experiences* and then watched the behaviour that
followed. This procedure was in marked contrast to that used by
Freud and Klein, whose conclusions were built up from the clinical
material gained during the psychoanalysis of their patients as
adults, and then extrapolating backwards, a process of work that
has proved to be dangerous. Interestingly, in Freud's early clinical
practice, he did indeed listen to the stories of some of his women
patients who spoke of their incestual experiences. These accounts
led him to see these experiences as the source of their so-called
"hysterical" symptoms. (From these, he developed his "seduction
theory".) Unfortunately, he was unable to hold on to this understanding that real life experiences were the cause of trauma,
especially in the face of a huge hostile response to his theory from

his colleagues. He then abandoned it and developed a different explanation for his patients' suffering. He came to the conclusion that the sexual abuse never really happened, but was purely a fantasy in the minds of his women patients as infants, who wanted to seduce their parent of the opposite sex. This led him to create the theory of the "Oedipal conflict" and "penis envy" and the notion that the cause of mental distress in the child comes from their having witnessed the "primal scene" (that is, sexual intercourse between the parents). The tragedy of this failure on Freud's part to stay with the recognition of how deeply traumatic these actual experiences of sexual abuse were for his patients contributed largely to the years of disbelief about the existence of sexual abuse, and incest in particular. It also led to the additional trauma and pain of thousands of children and adults whose experiences of abuse were rejected or ignored. This resistance to the real experiences of abuse has also influenced the school of thought that supports "the false memory syndrome".

Bowlby believed strongly that psychoanalysts in the past had placed far too much emphasis on "internal dangers" at the expense of actual external threats. Bowlby felt that it was as important for psychoanalysts to recognize the way children are *really* treated by their parents as it was for them to know what *perceptions* of their parents children held in their minds.

The phrase "a secure base" is a fundamental part of Attachment Theory. It is used to describe how Bowlby and other attachment theorists define what is available in childhood when children have had a secure attachment to their primary carers. Bowlby also uses it as a description of what attachment therapists attempt to create for their clients, recognizing that they have not had this at a time in their lives when they should have done so.

Mary Ainsworth, who worked closely with Bowlby in expanding Attachment Theory, wanted to create a way to diagnose whether babies were or were not "securely attached" to their primary carers. She devised what she called "the strange situation" experiment in order to do this (Ainsworth, 1978). This creates a way of observing objectively how a child of a year old reacts to separation from its mother and also from a stranger. A twenty-minute session is set up in a playroom with an experimenter in it. The mother comes in with her child and after a while she goes out of the room for three minutes, leaving her child with the experimenter. She then comes back in and joins her child again. After a while both she and the experimenter go from the room for another three minutes, leaving the child on its own, until the mother rejoins the child again. The whole process is videoed and the ratings of "security" or "insecurity" are based on how the child responds both to being left and to its mother's return. Four distinctive patterns of responses were identified, which were categorized as follows.

1. The "securely attached" child is generally distressed by the separation. It turns to greet its mother on her return, accepts comfort, and then returns happily to playing.
2. The "insecure–avoidant" child shows little distress as the mother goes and no great reaction to her return, especially when she comes back for the second time. Such children tend to stay observing their mothers and, as a result, remain inhibited in their play.
3. The "insecure–ambivalent" child is very distressed by her mother's leaving and difficult to comfort. Such children tend to display a need for closeness and comfort, but when this is offered, tend to express anger and kick any offered toys away. They remain inhibited in their play, as might be expected.
4. The "insecure–disorganized" child belongs to a category that has only recently been added. It is a small group of children whose responses are confused and unpredictable. Often such children would "freeze" on being reunited with their mothers.

This diagnostic tool has been used now for many years in different countries and is recognized as a valid one. The most important part of it is the similarities between the behaviour of mothers and their children. Thus, the categories in which mothers were located were mirrored in the categories into which their children were placed. The mothers of "securely attached" children tend to be highly responsive to them. Mothers of the "insecure–avoidant" children tend to be unresponsive. They may be mothers who never wanted a child, or who are deeply depressed and unable to respond. Mothers of the "insecure–ambivalent" children are those who behave inconsistently, so that their children never know what to expect. They will encourage their child one moment and ignore it the next. The mothers of "insecure–disorganized" children are those most likely to be suffering from severe emotional problems themselves and are more likely to have been sexually abused, or to have suffered from physical or emotional neglect, in their own childhood. The important conclusion from all this research is that the patterns of attachment, for every one of us, come from the *interaction* with our parents or primary carers. One of the interesting variants is when two parents or carers respond differently to their children, so that, for example, a mother may not be able to be responsive enough to make a secure attachment because of her own experience of early caring, but the father can, or vice versa. The conclusion that attachment theorists have drawn is that having one responsive parent is better than if neither is responsive, but, as one might expect, having two is definitely best.

➣ When all this work, with so much emphasis on the importance of maternal care, first became known it met with huge opposition, not only from other psychoanalysts as already described, but also from feminists. In the 1960s and 1970s so many younger women were struggling, often through joining "consciousness raising" groups, to find ways of freeing themselves from lives that were feeling very restricted. They were looking after babies and children with little sense of being valued for doing so, and with very little independence, financial or otherwise. To hear, as so many of them did, that Dr Bowlby (a man at that!) was apparently telling them that as mothers they should be not only available all the time, but also constantly responsive to their babies and children, seemed like the last straw. Such a reaction seemed very understandable at the time, but unfortunately it was mainly because many of them had not read Bowlby's work, but just listened to the general outcry and joined in. Bowlby has made it clear that it is not *routine care* of babies or young children that is so significant, but the ability of the mother to respond with *pleasure and encouragement to the child's social advances*, that really matters. Two feminist women therapists were honest enough to write an article (Brave & Ferid, 1990) in which they admitted that at first they were ill informed about Bowlby's views on maternal care, and that they had misunderstood what he had written. When they studied his work, they described how they came to appreciate the value of Attachment Theory in their own work as psychotherapists. It is, however, only fair to say that Bowlby did believe that mothers, on the whole, were better able to offer the sensitive, responsive care that babies and children need than were fathers. But he was a man of his time and this kind of judgement—that men of his generation were better kept out of close contact with small children—was probably accurate. It would have been almost unheard of that a father was present at his baby's birth[1] at the time when Bowlby was having his family, yet now it is commonplace. I think if he were alive today, he would be modifying his view. Some fathers may be more able to make secure attachments for their children than their mothers and, of course, this may always have been the case because, as Bowlby has so clearly shown, the ability to do this is due to their own experience of being sensitively parented. As it becomes more and more common for fathers to care for small children, so it will become easier for other fathers to feel more confident in playing a more intimate and sensitive parental role.

Another person whose researches led to the development of Attachment Theory was Mary Main. She devised a way of diagnosing "secure" or "insecurely attached" adults (Main *et al.*, 1985). This test, known as the "adult attachment interview" (AAI), is like a mini psychotherapy session in that it involves the person giving a lot of thought to their personal history, particularly their childhood. The person is asked to choose five adjectives that best describe their relationship with each of their parents during their childhood. Examples from actual memories have then to be given that "match" each adjective. After this, fifteen questions are put. Among these are questions that ask the person to give details about what each parent did if the child was upset, and which parent the person felt closest to as a child. They will be asked if they ever felt rejected or threatened by their parents and whether they have any explanation as to why the parents behaved as they did. Further questions cover whether the person thinks that their relationship with their parents has changed over time and asks if they think that their early experiences have affected their present way of behaving. This test takes quite a long time to do. Interestingly, the AAI generates four diagnostic categories that are very similar to those of the "strange situation" experiment. The first is "autonomous and secure", the second is "dismissing–detached", the third is "pre-occupied–entangled" and the fourth is "unresolved–disorganized". This test has now been widely used and its validity confirmed.

Above all, it has shown a strong connection between the attachment category of the parent and that of their child.

It is valuable to have this kind of knowledge confirmed by reliable tests, because it is the sort that is widely understood in straightforward terms: simply put, those adults who have had very poor, deprived parenting often find it very hard to parent their own children. Some such people make an enormous effort to parent, determined never to give the same cruel experiences to their children that they have had themselves. This is often done at a price; one mother described to me how very sad she felt at what she realized she had missed as she strove to be loving to her young children. Another woman went to the lengths of having an abortion rather than bringing a child into the world because she was so uncertain about her ability to love it, being so aware of the lack of love in her own childhood.

As the title of Bowlby's trilogy suggests, a further development of Attachment Theory came to him through his recognition of the part that *unwilling* separation and loss of attachment plays in creating our deepest emotional distress and feelings of anger and violence. He and his colleagues recognized that parents who ill-treated their children and deprived them of love, or who were physically present but not able to respond, left their children with a sense of tremendous deprivation, a form of long-lasting loss, leading to mental breakdowns or delinquent behaviour. This sense of loss, whether it comes from actual loss through death of a primary attachment figure, or the threat of loss from whatever cause, could, Bowlby believed, lead to emotional disturbances that could affect the person for life.

Such experiences drive children into seeking certain ways of behaving to deal with these feelings of loss, because they experience them as so overwhelming that they are sensed as intolerable. They are often pushed out of the child's conscious awareness and dealt with by denial. This is shown when adults who have actually had very emotionally deprived childhoods will say, as adults, that their childhood has been "all right" or even "happy". Some children, alternatively, will make desperate attempts to appease their parents. Others may be very aggressive; having felt themselves uncared for they will, in turn, care for no one. Still others may fall back into believing that if only they are "helpless" or "ill" enough, perhaps they will get the care they long for. For example, one person described how as a little girl she feigned not just illness but "being dead" in the hope that her mother would show delight on finding her daughter was alive after all. In reality, her mother scorned her for being "stupid". When she was really ill, this child felt she could not dare tell her mother for fear of being seen as an unbearable burden. *

These patterns of behaving are built up by the child in an attempt to keep intact their *inner sense of themselves*. But they rarely work. Furthermore, it is not surprising that such patterns can be very hard to change, and even harder to live with, when they persist into our adult lives. During the process of psychotherapy, such a person can come to recognize the huge resistance inside themselves to letting go of these sorts of patterns and slowly discovering a different and more liberating way of being.

There is now sufficient evidence to show that children brought up with "insecure attachments", particularly those in the "disorganized" category, who have been physically, sexually, or emotionally severely abused, can feel themselves deeply alienated from the rest of society. Such feelings make them highly vulnerable to further abuse, inflicted either by themselves, or by others. This may take the form of self harm, severe depression, or long-term anxiety. These are brought about because such people feel they are to blame for what has been done to them and feel that they are of no value. Equally seriously, they can be at great risk of antisocial behaviour and violence towards others. What is even more dispiriting is how our society reacts to such people through the ways many of our institutions are organized. This applies principally to our penal system, which demands retribution and punishments that simply recreate and sustain the person's sense of alienation.

When children commit serious crimes, particularly against other children, our society seems to give only limited recognition to the degree of deprived parenting such children have had. It is becoming increasingly important to recognize how much such children have already suffered and equally to appreciate the kind of deprived childhoods their parents have also had. What is now needed so urgently is to find ways of breaking these circles of emotional deprivation, alienation, and violence. Much more support needs to be given to parents who are unable to offer the kind of loving care that children need, but at the moment comparatively little money is spent on such programmes. Alice Miller (1990) suggests many ways societies could change if they recognized the role of attachment failures in the development of violence and mental disorders and used this knowledge in our social institutions.

One of the most interesting discoveries about the affect of separation of young children from their parents came about through the evacuation of thousands of children during the Second World War. Susan Isaacs and Dorothy Burlingham (1942) were the pioneers in this field. Children were sent off into the country to be safe from the bombing of cities. Yet a sense of "safety" that young children *perceive for themselves*, derives from staying close to their parents and *not* being separated from them. Mothers were not sent away with their children, because they were needed to do essential war work while their husbands were fighting. Importantly, one of the research findings was that small children, even in situations of great danger, showed little fear or anxiety provided they were with mothers who remained calm.

Further work on recognizing the impact of separation of small children from their mothers came when one of Bowlby's colleagues, James Robertson (1952), began to study how children behaved when separated from their mothers through being sent into hospital. He made a now famous film entitled *a Two-Year-Old Goes to Hospital*. It generated tremendous controversy among doctors and nurses, who had believed for years that they took sufficient care of their small patients. The film forced them to see how very distressed small children became when separated from home, and that even short periods of separation could have long-lasting effects. At that time, parents were allowed only very restricted visiting of their children in hospital and these children grieved, at first crying and often regressing in their behaviour, and ultimately sinking into uncomplaining despair, at which point they were quite wrongly perceived to have "settled down". It took many years of a huge campaign started by mothers, who knew instinctively that when their children were ill, the more they needed their mothers. Robertson's studies helped mothers and the more enlightened professionals to challenge the old restrictions when the research findings showed that separation from their mothers put the children's emotional health at risk, quite apart from the stress it caused their mothers. The campaign started as "Mother Care for Children in Hospital" and then changed to "The National Association for Children in Hospital". Over the years, and through an enormous amount of work on behalf of its members, there has been a huge shift in hospital policies so that now most hospitals that admit children have open visiting. They also allow mothers of small children to stay with them. There are play facilities and the presence of parents is seen as an integral part of the young child's treatment. It is perhaps one of the ways in which Attachment Theory has led to a big change in both attitudes and practice, thus making a real difference to the lives of many ill children and their parents.

Bowlby saw the role of the mother as "regulating" the extreme feelings of the child, by responding to him sensitively and consistently at times when he is frightened or overwhelmed by his feelings of anxiety, anger, or despair. In this way the child knows such feelings can be controlled or modified and comes to learn how to do this for himself. All the current neurological research now being done, largely through brain scanning, has shown that an inability of mothers to be able to reassure children in this way can actually lead to a failure of parts of the child's brain to develop. Children who do not have the stimulus and the response of a loving primary carer often show many deficiencies. Nothing shows this more horrifyingly than the extreme example of the brain scans of some Romanian orphans who have had no mothering at all. These children's scans show large gaps where their brains have failed to develop. Work done on examining the brains of less severely deprived small children shows up specific difficulties that come from a failure of brain development in the very early years. (See for example, Schore, 1994; Siegel, 2001.) These tend to leave such children unable to fully comprehend how others feel. They also tend to over-react to stressful situations and to respond to threatening situations by withdrawing.

Bowlby was the first psychoanalyst to highlight the significance of separation and loss of attachment figures for humans *of all ages*. He also said that the *fear* of separation is part of a human being's basic behavioural equipment. He claimed there is nothing "babyish" about this fear, suggesting that the separation from an attachment figure creates anxiety equivalent to that felt by the leader of an expeditionary force when he is cut off from base (Bowlby, 1988).

☞ As Bowlby studied people's reactions to loss, particularly bereavement of a primary attachment figure, he recognized four phases in the process of mourning such a deep loss. The first phase is one of feeling *numb*, almost without feeling. It carries with it a sense of disbelief and, for many, a sense of unreality. The second phase lasts much longer and is characterized by *yearning*, and *searching* for the lost person, accompanied generally by both crying and feeling angry. The bereaved person may be very restless, and also want to talk endlessly and in great detail about the way the person died, or deserted them. The third phase is one of *disorganization and despair* as the person feels overwhelmed by inner turmoil and not knowing how to cope, as they realize that the person they have lost is not coming back. This is the time when suicide is most likely to occur. The final stage is one of *detachment*, with the possibility of *reorganization* as the person slowly comes to terms with their loss and starts to find either new attachments or to strengthen old ones. These phases do not follow each other in a neat, consecutive way, but overlap. Other collaborators with Bowlby, such as C. M. Parkes (1964), who made a special study of bereavement particularly in relation to the loss of a spouse, have come to the conclusion that although depression does occur in some people who have been bereaved, it is not inevitable. It depends very much on the attachment pattern of the bereaved person, how they have reacted to other, previous losses, the nature of the relationship that was held with the person who has died or left, and also what other attachments are available at the time of the loss. For example, frequent broken attachments especially early in life, can lead to a state of permanent "detachment", when the person no longer seeks connections because of the pain that they have experienced in losing them. Bowlby described this as also happening in children who were never attached in the first place.

✦ As Bowlby developed his Attachment Theory, recognizing how human beings both seek attachments and react to their loss, he saw the relevance of the theory to therapy. He worked for many years applying the basic principles of Attachment Theory to effective psychotherapy. As he listened to the experiences of his patients, he recognized that talking about painful pasts was not easy. Thus, he sought to offer a "secure base", so that his patients felt safe enough to trust him, enabling them to share their dreadful experiences from the past and begin to perceive themselves as people of value. Above all, he sought to make a real relationship with them, minimizing the inevitable power differentials that exist between a therapist and his or her patients.

Attachment therapy is explored in more detail in other chapters of this book, so it needs no further coverage here. Ending on an optimistic note, it is important to recognize that whatever form of "insecure attachment" may have been one's lot in early life, none of us chose his or her parents. Their limitations were due to their own childhood experiences, and without blaming them or ourselves we can come to recognize that psychotherapy can enable people to change. Good experiences and the possibility of making new, more secure attachments certainly help as well.

CHAPTER TWO

Attachment and self-understanding: parenting with the brain in mind[1]

Daniel J. Siegel

Introduction

The word "attachment", and the idea that early attachments matter throughout life, can evoke a wide range of responses from parents, policy-makers, educators, and others concerned with how children develop. For some, it signifies a positive experience of the relationship between child and parent. For others, a sense of dread may emerge with the idea that somehow what has happened early in life will determine destiny without hope of liberation from patterns of the past. The old notion, a misinterpretation of the field of attachment research, is that our early life experiences somehow determine our fate without a chance for change. Such a view gives rise to a sense of hopelessness: What is the point of learning about attachment if it just tells you that you are helpless to make a change as an adult? The fact of the matter is that this fatalistic notion is wrong. Carefully conducted scientific studies have shown us that *it is not what happened to you that matters most in determining how you raise your children; instead, it is how you have come to make sense of your early life experiences* that is the most robust predictor of how your children will become attached to you.

Amazing, but true! In this chapter I will invite you to sit down with me and explore the wonderfully intriguing ideas and accessible practical implementations of the science of attachment.

In my own journeys through medical school and clinical psychiatry training and then into research into attachment, emotion, memory, and narrative, I have come to realize how central attachment relationships are in our lives. What has fascinated me over the past ten years, as we've come to understand more about how the brain develops and works, is how the objective findings from an array of sciences have deepened our understanding of the role that relationships play in our day-to-day subjective lives. Drawing on a wide range of scientific findings from, for example, anthropology, communications, social psychology, and neuro-science (like evolutionary biology and developmental neuroscience), we have arrived at ways of understanding the connections between our attachment experiences, and the development and function of the brain. This is an approach we call "interpersonal neurobiology" (Baron-Cohen *et al.*, 2000).

Why is interpersonal neurobiology relevant for parents? How does "parenting with the brain in mind" differ in any way from other approaches to helping parents raise children? Do parents really need to know about neurones to raise their children well? The answers to the first two questions, I hope, will be revealed as you read on. The last question about the brain can be answered simply: no. Parents do not need to know about the brain. Research has shown that parents do need to know about themselves, but not necessarily about neurones. However, I will suggest to you that having a mind filled with up-to-date knowledge about the science of human experience, including the neurobiology of the human mind, can prepare parents to understand both themselves and their children, and help all of them live, relate, and develop well.

When my book, *The Developing Mind* (Siegel, 1999), first came out, my daughter was in preschool and I was asked to give a few lectures on parenting and the brain. Mary Hartzell, the preschool director, attended along with the teachers and parents of the school. Mary is an early childhood educator renowned for her superb teaching abilities and her powerful approach to helping parents raise their children by giving respect to their unique experiences. Mary and I quickly realized that our approaches were very similar, despite our quite distinct professional backgrounds. The following year we organized a series of workshops for parents and teachers. Their response inspired us to integrate our perspectives in *Parenting from the Inside Out: How a deeper self-understanding can help you raise children who thrive* (Siegel & Hartzell, 2003). The "voice" of that book is directed to parents. Speaking frankly to the reader, it weaves stories together with personal invitations for self-reflection that are intended to help parents develop a more coherent understanding of themselves and their children. That understanding, we feel, is deepened when we can blend both subjective and personal reflections with objective scientific knowledge.

What science tells us about our interpersonal heritage

Developing the capacity to understand the minds of others

We can turn to neuroscience to understand more about our internal subjective and interpersonal social lives. Science has shown us that the brain has evolved as a social organ of the body. Mammals are social creatures, with structures called the "limbic" circuits that appear to serve the two purposes: they attune to the social environment while regulating the internal state of the body. The limbic regions help us understand the need in mammals for the presence of care-givers; *it is to help regulate the physiology of the young infant*. As that infant mammal grows, its ability to regulate its own physiology in a balanced manner will develop a more autonomous capacity in which the growing organism will become more independent of its parents for balancing its own internal state. Studies of maternal deprivation in rats and in monkeys have shown that permanent alterations in the behavioural and physiological response to stress strongly influence the capacity of the maturing animal to function socially. While infants can be seen in general as having the capacity to adapt, research clearly shows how early adverse experience can have negative effects on growing brains and persistent effects on functioning (Bremner, 2002).

As primates evolved, they were not only social and tuned into the state of others; they also evolved a mirror neurone system that enabled them to respond to the intentional (rather than random) acts of other members of the species. *Mirror neurones* represent a system that links perception to motor action (Hesse, 1999). When an intentional act is witnessed (such as the raising of a cup to drink), the same mirror neurone will fire as when the individual observing the act enacts that same behaviour. By responding only to intentional acts, and not just to random motion, mirror neurones reveal the ways in which our minds respond to the intentional state of another being.

Through our evolution as humans, we have taken the mirror neurones one step further into the world of representing in a more abstract way the internal state of others. This *capacity of having a sense of another's mind* has been called "theory of mind", "mentalizing", "mind reading", and "mindsight". The capacity for mindsight enables us to perceive the minds of others and to put ourselves in the "mental shoes" of another person, something other primates, though they have mirror neurones and can imitate, apparently cannot do. A number of authors (Hesse *et al.*, 2003) have suggested that this representational ability emerged at least 10,000–40,000 years ago; the evidence for this can be found in the representational art of the Palaeolithic era. Rather than just an interesting feature of our past, this mind capacity may have been the basis for our ability to create more abstract representations of the world beyond our social interactions. These emerging capacities may have been the origins of our human ability to consider various abstract possibilities, opening the door to cognitive abilities to manipulate the world of ideas, and objects, beyond our ancestors' wildest dreams. Such representational abilities enable us to communicate with each other in more complex ways and establish the process of cultural evolution.

Family relationships, communication and mental processes

When we move from a focus on the evolution of our species to the development of individuals in modern life, we can dive into the field of attachment research and ask how family relationships shape the genetically inherited capacity for various mental processes (Kandel, 1998). Attachment research is a field of developmental psychology that examines how patterns of communication between parent and child shapes the development of the child in various domains, such as in the social, emotional, and cognitive areas. Across all cultures studied a process called *contingent communication* is found, in which the signals of a child are perceived, made sense of, and responded to in a timely and effective manner. This sensitive form of care-giving enables the child to feel safe and understood, to know that its needs will be met, and that the parent is a reliable source of nurture and protection.

One can see the "A-B-Cs" of attachment (Kandel, 1998) as how the parent *Attunes* to the child, enabling her to achieve a sense of bodily *Balance* that then gives rise to a sense of *Coherence* internally and interpersonally (see Table 1). When parents generally provide a sense of *predictable contingency (with parents offering sensitive, perceptive, and responsive care-giving)*, the child feels understood, joined, and a sense of communion between parent and child is established. We can never provide the attunement that enables these A, B, Cs to be created all of the time—but we can offer communication and relatedness in a "good enough" manner, especially when our children are in need. Good enough means that we parent with the intention to respect the sovereignty of our child's emerging needs to be loved, to be understood, and to explore. It also means that when we miss such opportunities for connection and sensitivity to our child's evolving needs, we can make timely and effective repair of such inevitable ruptures.

The evolutionary benefit of the attachment system is that it motivates the infant to *seek proximity* to the parent, especially at times of distress, thus increasing its chances of survival. Beyond proximity seeking, the infant uses the parent as a *safe haven*, somewhere she can be soothed when upset. The infant then internalizes, as a *secure base within herself*, the relationship with the

Table 1. The ABCs of attachment
(adapted from Table V A from Siegel & Hartzell, 2003).

The ABCs of attachment are the developmental sequence of:	
Attunement	Aligning the parent's own internal state with those of the child, often accomplished by the contingent sharing of non-verbal signals
Balance	A child's attainment of balance of its body, emotions and states of mind through attunement with the parent
Coherence	The sense of integration that is acquired by the child through its relationship with its parents in which the child is able to come to feel both internally integrated and interpersonally connected to others

parent. This gives the child a sense of security that enables it to go out into the world to explore. Much of parenting is a balancing act between the child's need for closeness and his or her drive to explore the world. Parents may feel more comfort in one dimension than another, and this shapes the ease with which a parent can engage the child in intimate dependency and encourage more autonomous exploration.

Contingent communication promotes well-being and serves as a source of resilience to stress

Attachment research has demonstrated that parents, at least in the Western cultures studied, reveal characteristic patterns of communication with their children that promote specific forms of adaptation. With contingent communication, the child develops a *secure* attachment that promotes well-being and serves as a source of resilience to stress. With various forms of *non-contingent communication* (such as emotional distance or intrusiveness), the child may develop one of the so-called "insecure" forms of attachment. With an emotionally impoverished relationship, the child may develop an *avoidant* attachment, predictive of later difficulty in relating to peers and having a poorly-developed autobiographical sense of self. If the parents are inconsistently available for sensitive, contingent communication, then the child may develop an *ambivalent* attachment predictive of later uncertainty and anxiety in social situations. These two forms of insecurity from suboptimal parenting are adaptations to a child's family life that are useful, and organized, enabling the child to "do the best he or she can" given the circumstances. This organized form of adaptation is quite distinct from the next form of insecurity, called disorganized attachment.

When the parent is the source of terror and alarm, the child may develop a disorganized attachment predictive of later difficulty with social relationships and balanced emotional regulation. In this situation, the child cannot form an organized adaptation, but rather responds with a fragmentation of the self. Children with this form of insecurity have been shown to develop the clinical finding of dissociation in which normally associated cognitive processes, such as consciousness, emotion, and memory, become disassociated. Dissociation and social difficulties associated with disorganized forms of attachment are possible risk factors for developing posttraumatic stress disorder if an individual is exposed to an overwhelming event in the future. In this way, by the parent repeatedly creating a state of alarm in a child, especially without any hope of a safe haven, the child is presented with a "biological paradox": its brain motivates it to move toward the care-giver for soothing, but this parent is the very source of its alarm. This is what researchers Main and Hesse [1990] have called "fright without solution".

Self-understanding in parents: the adult attachment interview

Why would parents act in ways that were not helpful to their children? To answer this question, attachment researchers devised a set of questions called the adult attachment interview, or AAI, that asked parents to reflect on the nature of their own childhood experiences. The coding of this research instrument involves an analysis of not only what parents say happened to them, but also, more importantly, how they tell their story (Meaney, 2001). The AAI findings can predict, even in a pregnant couple, what kind of attachment their future child is like to develop with each parent (see Table 2). This finding supports the general notion that attachment is

Table 2. Attachment categories for children and adults
(adapted from Table VI A from Siegel & Hartzell, 2003).

Child	Adult
Securely attached	Free or autonomous (secure in approach to attachment)
Avoidantly attached	Dismissing (minimizes importance of attachment)
Ambivalently attached	Preoccupied or entangled (remains with leftover issues)
Disorganizedly attached	Unresolved trauma or loss/disorganized (unresolved issues lead to disorganization in the autobiographical narrative)

Adult attachment can be determined by how parents tell the story of their early life history to another adult. Parents' understanding of themselves is revealed through this adult-to-adult communication, not through how parents explain their early histories to their own children. The way the story is told, not merely the content, reveals characteristics of the parent's state of mind regarding attachment. These narrative patterns are associated with the child's attachment status to that parent as demonstrated in the above table. Long-term studies have further shown that adults" narratives generally corresponded to their own childhood attachment categories assessed decades earlier. An "earned secure" grouping exists in which adults have made sense of their lives and become free of what may have been a suboptimal experience of childhood. These adults have securely attached relationships with others.

a measure of a child's *experience*, not a function of genetics or other constitutional feature of the child. The AAI reveals that the characteristic way in which parents remember their past, the coherence of their autobiographical story, is actually the most robust predictor of the child's attachment to them.

What does the coherence of the adult's narrative actually mean? A coherent life story is one in which the adult has made sense of his or her own childhood experience and has insights into how that past has influenced his or her development as an adult and as a parent. Making sense is revealed in a flexible and reflective narrative that is predictive of that adult's child having a secure attachment. In contrast, a narrative without much access to autobiographical detail or sense of how the past influences the present, is associated with a parent of a child with an avoidant attachment. Parents with "leftover issues", emotional themes that intrude on the present attempt to tell the story of their lives, have children who are ambivalently attached to them. Children with disorganized attachment have parents with unresolved trauma or loss.

For clinicians, this latter finding raises a red flag of caution because disorganized attachment has the most concerning, negative outcome of all the groupings. Yet unresolved trauma and grief are treatable conditions. Disorganized attachment is thus likely to be a preventable condition. Helping parents resolve their unresolved trauma and grief may be a vital intervention in order to break the cycle of cross-generational transmission of disorganized attachments (Kandel, 1998). When Mary Hartzell and I created our integrated approach to parent education, we had in the front of our minds the importance of inviting parents to reflect on this and other aspects of attachment research in order to help their children develop well. By offering the opportunity to deepen self-understanding, to make sense of one's life, our hope is that parents could make the choice to enhance the security of attachment of their children while at the same time creating coherence and vitality in their own lives.

Beyond merely the idea of suboptimal attachments, the organized and disorganized forms of insecurity, lie conditions in which children are exposed to the overwhelmingly frightening events of child maltreatment. Disorganized attachment occurs in children who do not necessarily experience abuse. However, the majority of abused children have disorganized attachments. In the case of child abuse and neglect, recent studies have shown significant negative effects on the development of the brain. These studies have shown that the extreme attachment situation of child abuse and neglect is associated with several findings of brain damage, including an overall smaller brain size and damage to the fibres connecting the two sides of the brain to each other. Stress may damage the brain through elevated levels of the stress hormone cortisol, which is toxic to growing neurones (Bremner, 2002; Milad & Quirk, 2002).

Attachment and brain development

We can also look towards less extreme examples to explore the ways in which attachment may shape the developing brain. Recent studies in rats have demonstrated that maternal behaviour (i.e. licking the pups) actually leads to the stimulation of genetic information that shapes the way the infant rat's brain will develop. Differences in maternal behaviour directly influence gene expression that shapes the lifelong structure of the growing rat's brain (Schore, 2003). Studies in primates have shown that maternal interactions with young rhesus monkeys can lead to the normal development of the brain, whereas maternal deprivation can expose abnormal brain development in monkeys with particular genetic risks (Siegel, 1999). These studies confirm the general view in neuroscience that experience alters brain structure by the way in which genetic information becomes mobilized to alter connections among neurones in the brain. Future work will need to extend these basic experience–genetic principles to human subjects, but there is no scientific reason to believe that these general processes will not apply to our own species.

As discussed earlier, numerous independent studies converge on the view that the attunement of the parent to the child enables the child's brain to achieve bodily balance and later mental coherence. Born with a relatively small number of neural connections in the brain, the infant will have a massive increase in the complexity of neural connections shaped by both genetic information and by experience. We now know that experience shapes the brain by the following sequence: experience leads to neural firing that can activate genes that then lead to the production of proteins that enable the formation of new synaptic connections (Siegel, 2001; Siegel & Hartzell, 2003). It is likely, though not yet directly proven in human studies, that the experiences within attachment relationships shape the emerging neural circuitry of the child's developing brain. This shaping process, for example, may enable parent–child interactions to alter the genetically programmed ways in which the brain matures and sculpts those fundamental processes, such as regulating emotions, responding to stress, remembering our past, and even developing our abilities to empathize with others (mindsight).

Each of these processes is mediated in part by the important prefrontal regions of the brain, which develop during the first years of life (Suomi, 2003; Teicher, 2002). The prefrontal regions are *convergence zones*, which means that they integrate very different parts of the brain into a functional whole. This "neural integration" enables highly complex processes to emerge out of the differentiated functions of the brain (Iacoboni *et al.*, 1999). When differentiation is combined with integration, the complex system of the brain is able to function in highly adaptive, flexible, and stable ways. This is pretty much what we mean by the phrase "mental health". In this way secure attachment relationships may promote resilience and well-being by supporting the integrative capacities of the child's developing brain.

One proposal is that the parents who have made sense of their lives have achieved a certain degree of neural integration that allows them to be both internally coherent and available for interpersonal connections. When seen across the two sides of the brain, for example, such integration in a parent would mean that the logical, linear, and linguistic processes of the left side of the brain would be combined with the autobiographical, self-soothing, empathic processes of the right side (see Table 3). For the parent, the integration of the logical left and the autobiographical right sides of the brain could result in a self-understanding that makes sense of one's own life, a coherent narrative of life from the inside out. For a child, this would mean that the parent could find a way to use words to explore the subjective, internal world of the child's ongoing life experiences. Such an ability would make contingent communication quite likely to occur and may help explain how the

Table 3. Right and left modes of processing
(adapted from Table II from Siegel & Hartzell, 2003).

Right mode	Non-linear Holistic Visuo–spatial–analogic	Specializes in: Autobiographical information Sending and perceiving of non-verbal signals Intense and raw emotions Awareness, regulation and integrated map of the body Social cognition and mindsight: understanding others May involve a predominance of the brain's right hemisphere in processing
Left mode	Linear Logical Linguistic-digital	Specializes in: Syllogistic reasoning: looking for cause–effect patterns Linguistic analysis: using words to define the world "Right vs. wrong" thinking May involve a predominance of the brain's left hemisphere in processing

coherence of the parent's life narrative is the best predictor of the child's security of attachment.

Helping parents make sense of their lives

The exciting lesson from a range of sciences is that while experience shapes who we are, we are *not* destined to repeat the traumas of our past *if* we make sense of their impact on our lives. As parents, spouses, friends, and professionals, we can assist others in helping to make sense of their lives by supportive, empathic, emotionally meaningful, relationships that encourage authenticity and the nurturing of direct forms of compassionate communication. To do this, there are a number of basic things we can keep in mind as we try to make sense of what has happened in our own past and how this might influence the ways in which we communicate with our children.

1. Making sense of one's life involves being open to internal recollections that can enable them to become a part of a larger narrative of one's life. This is sometimes not a comfortable

process, but one that can yield a sense of vitality and openness to new possibilities. Becoming the author of one's own life story is the ongoing goal of the making-sense process.

2. Emotional communication between parent and child involves attuned communication that enables a parent to share and amplify positive emotions and share and soothe negative ones. Contingent joining creates a sense of emotional integration, a feeling that one is inside the mind of another. This sense of communion is at the heart of secure attachments.

3. Leftover issues can preoccupy parents' minds and interfere with the creation of a sense of joining between parent and child. Parents' defences can distort their accurate perception of their children's signals. Without self-reflection, such preoccupation can create a feeling of ambivalence within the child that may make them anxious to explore the world beyond their homes. Parents may inadvertently discourage a child's dependency, or drive towards autonomy without careful self-reflection and a deepening of self-understanding.

4. Emotionally disconnected patterns of earlier adaptation on the part of the parent may involve a blockage of a parent's access to his or her own right hemisphere processes (such as a sense of the body, raw emotions, self-soothing, autobiographical memory, and empathic understanding of others). Such a "way of being", if remaining unchanged, can be a source of impaired stimulation of the child's own right hemisphere. The resultant inhibition in the development of the right hemisphere's bodily, emotional, self-soothing, and interpersonal processes may shape the child's own development of a rigid pattern of avoidance in the world.

5. For parents with unresolved trauma or loss, patterns of interacting that have resulted in frightened or frightening behaviour with the child may be at the root of the development of the child's disorganized attachment with that parent. One proposal that may explain this process is the notion of a "low road of processing" that will be described in detail in the next section. In this state of mind, the usual higher, integrative functions that enable attuned empathic interactions are temporarily suspended. Coping with these terrifying states leads the child to develop a disorganized attachment. It is imperative that parents become aware of these processes and receive the support

they need to help reduce the low road's impact on children by moving toward the healing of their own unresolved issues.

The low road

The integration of clinical observations, parental reports, and neurological and neurobiological studies point to an explanation for how unresolved trauma and grief in a parent may produce the frightened, frightening, and in other ways alarming and disorienting parental behaviours that lead to disorganization in the child.

When the higher parts of the brain work in concert with the middle and lower portions, the brain achieves a highly integrated form of functioning. We can call this the "higher mode". This adaptive mode of processing links the cortical regions involved in thinking and executive functions with the limbic (emotion, memory, motivational) circuits and with the lower brainstem that brings in input from the body and regulates states of arousal. With such integration, the processes of reasoning, self-understanding, attuned communication, empathy, and morality are achieved. This higher mode can also be called the "high road".

In contrast to this adaptive and integrated state of mind, a "lower mode" of processing can occur, which involves a blockage of the higher regions from coordinating with the lower ones. In this "low road", the mind becomes inflexible and impulsively reactive without the benefit of self-reflection or empathic understanding. These states of mind can be triggered quite rapidly in response to "leftover issues" and triggers relating to unresolved trauma or loss. In this disconnected state of processing, we may engage in fearful behaviours that in other, higher, mode states, may have been extinguished (Wheeler et al., 1997). In this manner, functional disconnection of the higher cortical regions, especially the medial (middle) portions of what is called the prefrontal cortex, from other lower regions may release old fearful behaviours. Furthermore, a range of studies suggest that such a "low road" can temporarily suspend the higher processes of reasoning, self-reflection, attunement, empathy, and even morality.

Most of us have the potential to enter the low road. Certain conditions, such as being tired, hungry, or "at the end of our rope" may increase the likelihood of entering such a lower mode of response. One view is that unresolved trauma or grief involve the low road so that it (a) becomes triggered more easily, (b) is entered more rapidly, (c) when entered, remains longer, (d) involves more harmful behaviours, (e) is more difficult to recover from, and (f) when recovery occurs, repair of the disconnection—making a reconnection with the child—is less likely to occur.

An abrupt shift in the parent, who might otherwise be quite accessible and attuned to the child, would create a terrifying situation for the child. As we've discussed earlier, disorganized attachment does not only happen in abused children; non-maltreating parents may create disorganization in their child's attachment to them (Le Doux, 2002) perhaps by way of these low road behaviours. Low road interactions may terrify children and create the biological paradox of the attachment figure being the source of alarm. The innate drive of the child to move towards the parent for soothing is unable to be carried out as the parent is the source of the distress. If this state of being is not repaired by a parent re-entering the high road and creating a reconnection, it may be especially difficult for the child to make sense of these experiences. After repeated episodes of this type of confusing and distressful interaction, children with disorganized attachments develop impediments in their capacity to soothe themselves and to engage in flexible interpersonal relationships.

Healing old wounds and promoting secure attachments

Parents can learn to become aware of their low road experiences. Parents can be taught the steps to alter these patterns of entering the low road that create terror and generate disorienting disconnections for a child. It is imperative that we understand that even parents who have the best of intentions for their children, who love their children dearly, can have unresolved trauma or loss that makes them prone to these disorganizing low road behaviours. Parents with whom we work are profoundly relieved to gain insight into these otherwise confusing shifts in their mind's functioning, especially as they realize that they are *not* going "crazy" but instead are just normal people with unresolved issues. Previous shame and guilt can give rise to compassionate self-understanding that promotes changes in low road processes and enhances the parent's movement towards repair with the child.

Importantly, then, knowing about the brain can increase our understanding of our own emotional subjective and interpersonal lives. The simultaneous focus on parental self-understanding and patterns of interpersonal communication has offered a balanced and effective strategy to help parents promote secure attachments in their children. Bringing this knowledge to parents has been an exciting and profoundly rewarding experience.

Integrating knowledge from a wide array of scientific disciplines can help us understand development and the neural processes that give rise to the growing mind. We are still in the early stages of discovering the detailed ways in which relationships may help or hurt children's development. We know enough now from the independent fields of science to state that what parents do matters for children, and what parents do seems most influenced by how they have come to make sense of their lives. It is not just what happened to parents as children themselves that is the key, it is how parents have come to understand the impact of those events on their own lives that matters most. When parents have a compassionate understanding of themselves they are able to provide the emotionally sensitive, contingent communication that children need in order to thrive. While future research may deepen our understanding of the specific mechanisms by which relationships promote mental health, for now we can build on the emerging view of the "social" brain to help others and improve life across the generations.

Note

1. This chapter is based on the ideas explored in *The Developing Mind: How relationships and the brain interact to shape who we are* (Guilford, 1999) and *Parenting from the Inside Out: How a deeper self-understanding can help you raise children who thrive* (with Mary Hartzell, Penguin Putnam, 2003) and summarized in part in the article, The mind, the brain, and human relationships (*Gynaecology Forum International*, 2003).

CHAPTER THREE

Education for what? Attachment, culture and society

Marci Green and Marc Scholes

H uman society is made by people. As infants, we seek attachment with our primary care-givers for our comfort and security. This intimate environment of conversation and exchange is our first contact with the world "out there". That world is the larger environment inhabited by others, whom we gradually come to meet through family, neighbourhood, jobs, and community. These social settings influence the abilities of our primary care-givers to meet our needs, but they are also part of the wider social networks in which we come to live as children, adolescents, and adults.

We are social beings who think, feel, and do things in relation to others, and these relationships make life and society possible. Through these relationships, we develop a sense of self. This happens first through our intimate, face-to-face exchanges with our primary care-givers, and then through our wider connections with others. In the course of our development, we take into ourselves (internalize) many of the values and beliefs of our culture, as we learn what are considered appropriate ways of thinking and behaving in the society in which we live. This knowledge then becomes part of our sense of self. Ideally, there will be a comfortable fit between our sense of self, the expectations of others, and the rules of membership in the wider society, *particularly if our social institutions and culture can meet our attachment needs*. But, what happens if our social institutions and culture fail to do this; if the dominant values and expected ways of behaving are at odds with our need to seek and maintain secure attachments? *This conflict—between our need for secure attachments, and the values that societies generate and reward— threatens the mental health of individuals and communities.*

In this chapter, we will argue that the most rewarded values and behaviours in our society are, indeed, often in conflict with, and undermine, the recognition that attachments matter for life. This is the case in all our social institutions. Here, however, we will look at the culture, organization, and management of educational institutions to explore this conflict more fully.

Attachments, culture and society

Attachment Theory has largely focused on our *biological* capacities to attach to our primary care-givers, and the effects of attachment experiences on brain function and emotional abilities to form future attachments as we grow. This theory, therefore, is especially concerned with the biological needs for secure attachment, and the earliest environment in which these should—but might not—be met; this is the world of intimate, face-to-face relationships. However, since such relationships operate within wider social, economic, and cultural settings, we need to bring culture and society into our discussion.

Let's explore this idea more fully. What lies in the heart of Attachment Theory is the belief that infants biologically need their primary care-givers to meet two essential conditions. *They are that their primary care-givers be properly present, and be responsive to the needs of the infant in an appropriate way.* A primary care-giver's ability to meet these conditions depends importantly on their own early attachment experiences. However, it also depends significantly on their perceptions of what is appropriate behaviour towards their children and towards others with whom they relate. Those perceptions are powerfully shaped by the values and beliefs of our culture, the behaviour of those with whom we relate, and our understandings of what matters in life. These all influence a caregiver's own sense of self and, in turn, their ability to provide their children with the experiences necessary for secure attachment.

One helpful example of the link between emotional development, culture, and society is found in the work of Alice Miller. In her book, *For Their Own Good* (2001), she explores the popular philosophies and practices in Germany that influenced child-rearing for well over two centuries. These teachings—which she refers to as pedagogies—were designed to help guide parents through the uncertainties of raising their children, and although they expressed contemporary conventional views about what children needed to become responsible adults, she thought they influenced children and adults in poisonous ways. These pedagogies were largely punitive and repressive, as children were seen by their nature to be, out of control. Punishment was advised to keep them in order, and the soothing of pain was considered a dangerous indulgence. Such practices, Miller argues, injured the child's sense of self and the capacity to express his or her needs, but their impact was not limited to the individual personality. They helped prepare generations that yearned for love and regard to embrace the all-powerful source of authority that was Hitler.

Miller's message is clear: that there is a close connection between the cultures and societies in which we live and the kinds of human beings we become. She is not alone in this recognition, as others have made similarly compelling arguments. In this chapter, we want to borrow from their insights to reflect on the ways that our culture and institutional environments influence our abilities as parents to enable our children to feel securely attached. In particular, we want to suggest that there are strong influences within our culture that actively devalue human connection, and encourage and reward behaviour that separates us from others.

Attachments, culture and relational living

The term "culture" has a variety of meanings. It may be understood to refer to "high" artistic forms such as ballet, opera, or sculpture. The use of the term in this way suggests culture as something rare or uncommon and implies that only a small educated social elite is able to appreciate cultured events and pastimes. A different definition (and the one in which we are interested here) understands culture as all that is learned through human communication—values, beliefs, symbols, and rituals—whose meanings we come to share. This is everyday, lived, or common culture. It encompasses how we communicate and relate with each other, our leisure activities, the clothes we wear, our variety of customs and social practices, and so forth.

We learn the meaning of our shared culture through inter-personal communication, and by exposure to the values of our social institutions such as families, schools, the media, and the workplace. In this way, we develop the capacity to understand others and to have them understand us. This happens in all social groups, spans geographical boundaries and operates across generations. Often those values and meanings are so much a part of the fabric of our everyday life that we tend not to think about their cultural and symbolic significance. But, even though we may be unaware of them, they still shape our behaviour and emotional development in profound and complex ways.

It is the case that features of our culture can cause injury to individuals and groups. We can see this in the obvious examples of sexism, racism, ageism, and homophobia. These belief systems categorize people, diminish our integrity, undermines self-worth and inhibit the flow of mutual, value-giving human interaction. The processes by which such injuries occur, and their consequences for our ability to relate with others in a life-empowering way, have been the focus of much of the work by clinicians and researchers at the Stone Centre in Wellesley, Massachusetts. They describe their approach as a Relational/cultural model for understanding human growth and development.

While their approach differs in some respects from that of Attachment Theory, both schools of thought share the important idea that one's emotional and mental health requires connection with others. They challenge the popular view that the healthy individual is one who seeks separation from others in order to be independent, and argue, instead, that what really matters for human growth and mental health are mutually empowering relationships.

We can draw on the insights of the Stone Centre to explore how our culture and social institutions may limit our capacities to relate, (and, ultimately, our ability to provide secure attachments for our children). So, for example, Jordan (1999) and others (e.g. Hartling & Sparks, 2002) argue that deep-rooted within our culture are some strongly held assumptions about the qualities we should possess to be deemed successful members of society. Among these qualities are individualism, competition, and the rule of reason over emotion. We learn to think that if we have these qualities, they will help in our search for the right job, the best relationships, high social status, and the power to get what we need for ourselves—even at the expense of others. These qualities are, as the Stone Centre describes them, *non-relational*. That is, they undervalue connection and encourage the belief that separation is a condition for human development. It is also the case, however, that our culture encourages other qualities, ones which are *relational* in character because they encourage cooperation, mutual empowerment, and sensitivity and regard for the needs and feelings of others as well as ourselves.

One of the practical difficulties we all face is figuring out which qualities are appropriate to what social situation, but this, too, we learn—often through trial and error. By and large, we are encouraged to show caring, regard for others, cooperation, and mutual respect in the *private* spheres of family and friends, and in those professions that we single out as caring, but embrace individualism, competition, power, and "rational" calculation in our *public* lives (although many family relationships between adult partners, and between adults and children, are competitive, calculating, and abusive). Importantly, within our culture, the qualities we display in public life are the ones that are rewarded with high income, honour, prestige, and esteem. Particular *public* roles, such as sports and media celebrities, politicians and corporate executives, enable individuals to utilize these non-relational particular attributes to their economic and social advantage. These individuals can be highly rewarded for their performance even if their behaviour or economic decisions devastate families and local and national communities.

In contrast, those activities that require the use of relational skills such as parenting, caring for vulnerable members of society, nursing, and teaching are typically poorly rewarded by society.

Indeed, parents who wish to stay at home to bring up their children are encouraged to leave their children in day-care and return to work. This pressure is partly cultural, since work is an important source of social and self esteem, but it is also economic, as our society increasingly requires two incomes to help meet the sharply expanding consumer needs of the household. A man we met recently told us that he had to abandon a personally rewarding nursing career—something he cared about greatly—simply because it did not generate enough income for his growing family.

In these circumstances, what cultural messages are being conveyed to us about the qualities most valued in our society? And what impact do these messages have upon our ability to recognize the essential role of attachments in our lives? How do we learn to live well with others, in societies that undervalue the importance of connection for our health and long-term survival? In the terms of the Stone Centre's approach, how do we live relationally, in a non-relational world?

Against attachment and connection: three myths up close

It is worth looking more closely at the ideas developed by Stone Centre colleagues. Those ideas provide a useful context in which to understand much of the thinking and practice that is now shaping British social institutions. Although their work deals primarily with the United States, we believe their arguments apply to Britain.

Jordan (1999), Fletcher (1999) and Hartling and Sparks (2002) explore some powerful myths of American culture. We want to look at just three of them.

Hyper-individualism

One of these myths is hyperindividualism—an extreme form of individualism in which the human being is more valued *out-of-relation* than *in-relation*, more *against-others* than *with-them*. Hyper-individualism celebrates an exaggerated kind of independence as a measure of emotional and intellectual maturity, and equates connection with dependence, weakness (and women).

Competitive competence

Related to hyperindividualism is the Competition Model of Competence. Jordan reminds us that the words competition and competence have common Latin roots, and once conveyed a sense of "striv(ing) after (something) *in company*" (Jordan, 1999). This is not our current understanding of "competition", since it is now something we do *against*, rather than *with*, others. Jordan argues that the ability to compete (usually expressed as competitive individualism) is a popular way of judging someone's competence. We make these judgments because we believe, for example, that competition gets the best out of people; competition honours "the expert"; the individual succeeds by mastering things and people; competitive individualism makes us self-sufficient. Hence, we compete for money (my reward for a greater knowledge and livelier performance than yours), for prestige (I am the expert and have therefore earned it), for leadership (I developed my qualities all by myself, and in me resides ultimate authority), and for power (I have this over you, to make you do what I want because I can force you). This competitive model of competence is a myth in three ways. First, it fails to recognize that competition depletes our emotional resources and generates a culture of failure. Second, it conceals the truth that the real source of our energy, zest, and mutual empowerment is good connection. Third, the myth hides the truth that behind every alleged individual success is an army of people—some we know, others we don't—who help make it happen.

Hyper-rationality

A third myth of our cultural and institutional life is the belief that people are most effective in their relationships if they can rationally calculate which means will serve what ends. In Jordan's terms, this can take the form of *hyper-rationality*. This myth presumes that reason is separate from (and in conflict with) emotion, that emotion is dangerous and disorganized, and that the only things in life that matter are those things that can be measured.

These three myths, we believe, are also embodied in a kind of *accountancy logic*, which drives much current thinking and practice in our public institutions, not to mention in our intimate relationships as well. It is a logic perhaps best summed up by the idea that the only things that matter are things we can measure. So, how do these myths operate in our social institutions, and what are the implications of a non-relational culture for our abilities to make and maintain secure attachments?

Reflections on education

We have suggested that the dominant and most rewarded values and behaviours in our society are very often those that conflict with and undermine the recognition that the good connections (and attachments as a particular kind of connection) matter for our mental and emotional health. We want to apply their insights to recent developments in the British educational system to explore the conflict further, and reflect on the implications of this conflict for our capacity to make and maintain secure attachments. By way of introduction, let's consider an example of this conflict in a commercial workplace setting, and then turn to the matter of education.

A friend recently told us how it was common practice where he worked for a time as a sales executive for colleagues to delete each other's telephone messages, and destroy important sales request faxes in order to stop workmates from getting ahead in the sales tables. Individuals would also find ways to keep the office secretaries "sweet" in order to protect their backs and secure any possible advantage over colleagues. At the heart of this aggressive and uncollaborative environment we see operating a competitive model of competence linked to financial incentives.

Despite attempts to meet *team* targets, everyone understood that the priority was one's *personal* sales figures; the workplace ethos exemplified in the saying, "You're only as good as your last sale". At the end of the sales cycle the performance tables would be wiped clean, so the competition could begin again. Be near the bottom of the sales table too often and you would lose your job; maintain a place at the top of the table and you would be rewarded with status and increased influence in the office and, of course, bonuses, gifts, and even holidays. This firm encouraged a hyperindividualism that actively discouraged the opportunities for building relationships of trust with colleagues. The only thing that mattered was to meet the short-term sales targets, get ahead, and win bonuses for singular performances. How much business was lost to the company through telephone messages and faxes that were delayed or went unanswered was never calculated. Instead, this seemed to be ignored as some form of collateral damage. The company may have considered the human cost of the workplace culture, since staff so often came and went before they could even learn the job (and its tricks) properly. But the company's ethos did not change. Employees were seen as disposable assets whose only significance was economic.

We can speculate that this workplace culture is not uncommon to commercial enterprises and that it reflects ways of managing employee performance in a profit-driven environment. In this instance, sales is a key factor in determining the viability of a company operating in a market economy, and it is easy to see how all three myths, and an accountancy logic, influence company behaviour. However, would we expect the same values to operate in institutions whose avowed responsibility is the well-being of the community? Probably not. But, certainly over the past twenty years, the myths we have described have come to dominate British institutions involved in health, education, and welfare provision.

For example, there is evidence that both the organization and management of education in England have become increasingly individualist, rationalist, and competitive. These qualities do not just provide the basic framework for the operation of the institutions. They are seen as desirable qualities to which staff and pupils are encouraged to aspire. We believe, however, that they undermine the ability of staff to meet the needs of students, and reward non-relational values amongst pupils.

A colleague of ours recently described an experience in which the head of a primary school had been evaluated for his performance over the past year. The evaluation procedure was part of the school's broad policy on quality assurance and had to be strictly followed. It was also the basis on which bonus payments to the head teacher would be made, if his performance satisfied the necessary criteria. Our friend was struck by the fact that despite the procedure's ultimate aim to benefit the pupils and the school, omitted from the process was any mention of the emotional needs of the pupils. Instead, the focus was solely upon the role of the head teacher in the administrative operation of the school, specifying aspects such as "performance management policy", "vigorous monitoring", "creative management of budgets" and "strategies to raise standards".

It is important to know, too, that a special vocabulary had been created to accompany the evaluation procedure, and the procedure had to ensure that the relevant performances could be measured and evidenced *on paper*. Despite the large number of pages that the whole process generated, their contents could be boiled down to two key concerns. The first was about operating the school budget, and the second was about pupil performance in a national, statutory system of assessment. Important as these areas were for the management of the school, our friend thought there should have been room to address the quality of pupil's emotional experiences and development. Surely this must be important for our children's schooling?

However, it is easier to measure pupils' performance than their mental health and development. It is not that schools ignore the emotional life of their students, but attention goes to those with acute behavioural problems. Emotional well-being, then, is a matter of crisis management, not a routine goal of the general curriculum. What matters more is performance, and performance can be calculated. Amongst other things, this is what generates a school's resources. All pupils in England have to sit national tests, and their scores are used to judge the quality of the schools they are attending. School test results are then published in the local newspapers so that parents can make informed choices about which school will provide their child with the best education. The educational process, now, has to be reduced to qualities that can be numerically expressed. Municipal administrators, school governors, and teachers come under enormous pressure to enhance their pupils' test scores because they know their schools will be publicly ranked and evaluated in terms of the results.

The publication of school league tables has become a key feature in media coverage of education. Ostensibly about enhancing quality and enabling parents to make informed choices in selecting their school (ideas which are also rooted in the operation of market forces within education), the tables actually give no account of the lived experience of the pupils themselves. Furthermore, league tables maintain a competitive model of competency, by pitting school against school solely in terms of how well their pupils have performed. Through the evaluation procedure we described earlier, the management culture of the school has been modelled to reflect this obsession with competition, hyper-rationality and the underlying accountancy logic.

There are other worrying effects of managing education in this way. For one thing, the emphasis on performance outcomes does not take into account the unequal cultural and emotional resources that pupils bring into the classroom, despite the fact that such resources do matter to a pupil's learning process. Then, too, the children aged seven and upwards are put under excessive pressure to produce the results the teachers, parents, the school, and the school system are seeking. In addition, the tests exclude the more expressive subjects such as art, dance, music, and sports, and focus solely upon the academic subjects of mathematics and English. This conveys to pupils a limiting hierarchy of value, which might undermine the confidence of those pupils who are less academically able in maths and English. Ironically, then, the accountancy logic that fuels the machinery of quality in schools may fail to give pupils what they need and may even lead to behaviour that excludes them from the educational system.

Overall, what has now come to dominate British education is a culture of competition and performance, with its emphasis on measurement and uniformity. Emotional health and relational skills are fairly low on the educational agenda. Of course, pupils may well develop these qualities despite the formal curriculum, since much of our capacity to connect effectively is formed from a child's earlier attachment experiences. Also, a good personal relationship with a supportive teacher, and schoolmates, may help a child cope with the experience of insecure or failed attachment. But a child's secure base within him or herself, and the ability to relate well with others, should not be left to chance. Given the formative nature of the educational process, we have a collective responsibility to meet the relational needs of our children.

British Higher Education

These developments within the primary school sector in England, (and it is not dissimilar to the experience in many other "developed" countries) are mirrored in British Higher Education (community colleges and universities). Trends over the last two decades reveal a similar sharp shift towards a performance culture. Furthermore, Higher Education increasingly operates within the commercial sphere through the introduction of industrial logics and commercial values.

These trends are worrying. Although education has long been about social regulation, control, and preparation for the labour market, we think that Higher Education should continue to promote—as it once did—the less directly vocational values such as self-understanding, flexibility of mind, openness, the process of learning for learning's sake, and personal fulfilment. To achieve these objectives requires, we think, some protection from strictly market pressures. While we recognize that vocational training and appropriate preparation for the labour market are essential, we must also encourage students to develop relational skills and self-understanding. That these are not at the top of the educational agenda derives in part, we believe, from those political and economic processes that place markets before people, individual competition before cooperation and reason before feeling.

Since the 1980s, successive governments have argued that an increase in the proportion of those going into Further or Higher Education is an important factor in the economic (read competitive) success of Britain on the global stage. Consequently, these political leaders (who are under their own pressures to have quantifiable performance measures that can be fed to the media) have identified this as an indicator of their political performance. The current target for the year 2010 is that 50% of young people should carry on their education beyond the current compulsory age of 16.

The number of students entering study for a higher degree has increased significantly since the 1980s, as staffing numbers (and salaries) have lagged behind. This development has put intense pressure upon universities to cut the cost of educating people to degree level while struggling to maintain standards. In order to cope with this influx of students in such a short space of time, most universities have had to adopt industrial-style production processes and values. In effect, what has taken place in Britain is the massification of Higher Education not too far removed from the assembly line production models of Henry Ford.

The crucial industrial-style mechanism introduced by universities to teach large numbers of students has been the adoption of the American credit accumulation system. Academic programmes of study are now broken up into small, nugget-sized learning modules. Students select their modules from their institution's market place, and then accumulate the right number and type of credits to obtain their qualification. On the one hand, this development opens up a wide range of possible "learning packages" and enhances the universities' marketing strategies by appearing to offer choice and flexibility of study. Furthermore, government funding for universities is connected with their recruitment success. In these respects, then, the modular system has become central to the organization and management of learning and teaching in many Higher Education institutions. It also exerts a significant influence upon the culture of these learning environments—the lived experiences of staff and students.

While the appeal of student choice in selecting their programmes is tremendous, there are costs. One of the key characteristics of modules is the uniformity imposed on the teaching programme as a result of the need to measure student progress. Each module, therefore, must identify and define what are called learning outcomes. These are broken down into quantifiable criteria, specified well before teachers and students even meet each other in the classroom, and they form the basis upon which judgements about student performance are made. Its strength is that it provides an administratively logical and systematic approach to the processing of large numbers of students and grades; its weakness is that it ignores the individual student experience. To suppose that the learning outcomes for 200 students on a module can be measured in identical terms is clearly inadequate in human terms; students have different backgrounds, potentials, and interests.

The accountancy logic in Higher Education makes spreadsheets of all those creative processes that real learning entails, and charts an individual's self-growth on grids of performance targets. As university lecturers ourselves, we have seen colleagues struggle to measure something as fundamental as student contributions to seminar discussions. This was hard to do because it was so difficult to quantify those judgements that are qualitative by nature. It also undermined our belief that our judgements could be trusted without a quality-performance system to oversee our conduct. That we manage to work with students in a positive relational way at all is a real achievement, and we often succeed. But we do this despite, not because of, the system.

Concluding comments

We have argued that the myths of hyper-individualism, competition and hyper-rationality, operate at all levels of the education system. We are not surprised, given the economic impulses towards rationality, accumulation, and consumption that inform all our institutions and culture.

But why are we concerned? After all, however *non-relational* is the organization and culture of education, our students do graduate from our institutions with their proof of performance and, on the whole, do better in the labour market than those without degrees. Is this not, therefore, some measure of success? And, if so, why change the system if the system works?

As teachers committed to relational values, and the recognition that secure attachments—so essential for self and species survival—are influenced by our cultural and institutional environment, we believe that although we may educate our students to work well for the system, the system may not serve their mental and emotional development. For example, we are now witnessing real tension between our students' emotional needs and the myths that underpin the organization. One indicator for this can be found in a growing retention crisis as universities are struggling to keep students on their courses. Although there are numerous causes for the increased drop-out rate, our experiences with students incline us to place high on the list, the conflict between their relational requirements and the values of the system. Evidence for this comes from the acute pressure on lecturers and other colleagues to provide extensive remedial and counselling support for students. The resources to provide this support are woefully few, and we do the best we can. Perhaps if emotional distress were easy to quantify, more resources would be available. But we think the real causes lie elsewhere.

They reside, we believe, in the wider cultural and institutional settings in which education operates. In the Stone Centre's terms, we live in a non-relational world whereby relational messages can barely be heard above the din of competition, individualism, and hyper-rationality. And it is this environment that may hinder our ability to make and maintain secure attachments. Our culture and social institutions will influence how present and appropriately responsive we are for our children, and for others in our communities. Given the significance of attachments for human survival, at what cost do we ignore this truth?

CHAPTER FOUR

Attachment theory and ageing

Joan Woodward

I n Victorian times the prescription for children—now thankfully blown away—was that they should be "seen but not
heard". In our society today, elderly people are neither "seen"
nor "heard" in the sense of being fully valued, or perceived as
playing any worthwhile role. This attitude to elderly people not
only denies their attachment needs, but by and large makes it
impossible for them to be met. It contradicts the core belief within
Attachment Theory that attachment needs are vital from "the cradle
to the grave". This chapter attempts to raise some of the reasons
why the elderly are seen in this way. It particularly emphasizes how
the cultural issue of sexism so strongly influences the different way
ageing is experienced by men and women. It goes on to explore the
different stages of ageing, with the inevitable ageist attitudes that
accompany them. Finally, it suggests how the attachment needs of
the elderly could be put into practice in the area of housing, which
would reflect the change in attitude that is so desperately needed.

The vital role of early attachments and the influence of cultural issues

Bowlby, in his formulation of Attachment Theory, did not directly address the issue of gender. He chose to study attachments within the mother–child relationship, in animals as well as humans, to establish that attachment is instinctive, regardless of species. He recognized how attachment to a primary figure in childhood and adolescence operates at an instinctive level, because it is vitally needed for protection from predators for survival. He also emphasized the fundamental need of this relationship, offered in a sensitive way, because it enables the child to get a sufficient sense of a "safe self" to, as he put it, "explore" the world. This was the challenging new aspect of Attachment Theory that brought him so much criticism from his contemporaries, because it challenged previously proposed theories of human development. Bowlby and his many followers have continued to observe how deeply we are all affected by the nature of our parenting, not only as children, but throughout our adult lives. This is largely due to the patterns of behaviour that everyone of us sets up as *a result of our interaction* with our parents and other early attachment figures. These patterns continue to determine how we relate to others for the rest of our lives.

Through his many observations, Bowlby was able to show that the ingredients in attachments in early life that really matter are the *proximity* and *availability* in a *responsive manner* of our primary attachment figures. He stressed the importance of our primary figures being both around for us and responsive to us when we are young, because he recognized that the mere physical presence of a primary carer was not enough for a child to gain a secure attachment. If primary figures are so depressed or emotionally frozen that they cannot relate sensitively to their child or, worse, are actually abusive, this results in the child becoming "insecurely attached", with many subsequent problems. What now needs to be added to this important understanding is the recognition that parents, as people, are deeply affected by the prevailing attitudes of sexism and racism in our society. These may play a big part, not only in the way parents may have experienced being parented themselves, but how subsequently they parent their own children. Many parents may not even be aware of how much they are affected by these cultural attitudes and the important part they may play in the way they treat their children.

The importance of attachment figures throughout life

The two factors of *proximity* and *availability* of our attachment figures that Bowlby stressed continue to play an enormous part in the lives of older people, providing not only a sense of security, but also a continuing ability to "explore". This means to reach out to others, to lead as full a life as possible and to retain a sense of value of oneself, regardless of physical decline. This *recognition* of the profound significance of attachment figures continuing to be available throughout our lives, (even though these figures change in time) is of utmost importance to older people. Such a concept had never been proclaimed before in this way. It is a striking fact that, although there is knowledge of the attachment needs in older people, today's society rarely accepts it fully or acts upon it. I believe that the failure to do so is the cause of great loneliness, sadness, and grief for some elderly people, which affects both their physical and mental health.

In her well-researched study, Friedan (1994) showed that what men and women need in their life as they grow older is primarily *choice*, so that they can play a part in determining their lifestyle as far as it is possible to do. This is surely true for all ages, but so often denied for the elderly. All her researches showed that older people were happiest when they were in close contact with other people similar to themselves, with whom they could feel safe and have a sense of purpose in their lives. She describes many different types of communal living in the USA that offer elderly people ways of sharing their lives. When these are successful, there is a very high level of well-being among those involved.

Patterning from early attachment experiences.

One of the core understandings of Attachment Theory is that the patterning established in early childhood due to the type of "secure" or "insecure attachment" the child experiences, tends not only to last a lifetime, but in many instances can be very difficult to alter. As already described in the introductory chapter, it is "insecure attachments" and *unwilling* loss of attachments, that lead to a huge variety of emotional disturbances. As the research done by Ainsworth *et al.* (1978) and Main *et al.* (1985) showed, those adults who are unable to respond appropriately as parents to their children have, in their turn suffered either abuse at the hands of their parents, or severe emotional deprivation, or very inadequate parenting. Many of them, as Bowlby described, have had to "parent their parents', leaving them still seeking parenting for themselves. Such people often appear outwardly to be successful adults, yet they may at times be aware that part of themselves holds feelings of still being "needy children". This may lead to the person concerned struggling to keep such feelings out of awareness, which is often not wholly successful. They often act in very inappropriate, demanding ways.

When these children who have had to "parent their parents" become adults, they sometimes have a compulsive need to take extra care of their children, as well as other people. This is often done in ways that are determined by their own overwhelming need to demonstrate the importance of "caring", which deep down they feel they never had. Sadly, this kind of caring is rarely very agreeable to anyone on the receiving end, and the person giving it is also unlikely to feel good. People driven by compulsive caring are often left with feelings of resentment and sadness, believing, too, that they are never properly appreciated. They tend to deny their own needs because they do not believe these will, or can, ever be met. This is generally due to their concluding that it was their "greediness" in the first place that was the cause of their early deprivation. They are fearful of exposing a need that always feels "too big". Such people can at times go to extraordinary lengths to demonstrate their independence and are sometimes very hard to help. This can be a particularly sad way to be in old age, when there may be a real need for extra care, especially of a physical kind. In this situation, the person who needs it the most sometimes appears to be the least able either to ask for it, or to cheerfully accept it. Their deep feelings that people will perceive them as "undeserving", and that they will never get the loving care that they seek, often leaves them with a deep pain and anger, although they may not recognize the cause of it. It will tend to make them say such things to a carer as "I bet you wish you hadn't come", as soon as they enter the door!

The choice of rejecting care

Those who care for the elderly really need to understand this way of behaving and the source of it, because it is commonplace and so frequently misunderstood. If we have not been given the love and care that we *really needed and should have had* in early childhood, we often tend in later life to reject in one way or another any love or care that is offered to us. This is because we do not trust it, or fear that if we dare to do so, it will be unreliable and either disappear or be "taken away". It feels safer *not to have it* rather than expose ourselves again to the experience of loss that in the past felt so unbearable.

Survival strategies

Small children are often amazingly brave in the strategies that they are compelled to develop in an attempt to solve the unbearable experience of being deprived of parental love and care. Yet it is these very strategies, acted out over and over again throughout life, that tend to make it so hard for such people to find other versions in their later life of the "secure base" that Bowlby describes as the base we all need to live our lives as secure adults.

Many people want to believe that children whose childhoods have been very unhappy will be able to find a sense of security as they grow up. This may indeed happen to some who are lucky enough to find a person in their lives whom Miller (1991) describes as an "enlightened witness". This is someone who enables the child (and that may be the "child" within the adult) to realize that their feelings of "always being wrong" or "at fault" in some way does not belong to them, but has come from the environment in which they were raised. Many children never find such help and these patterns of thinking about themselves then tend to stick with them all their lives. Some people may be quite scornful about how events in early childhood can possibly have any affect on them in later life. They tend to say, "But those things happened very many years ago; they have no relevance now." Their way of dealing with the cruel or painful experiences that may indeed have happened to them very much earlier is to deny them, to keep them out of awareness and in this way to "forget" the terrifying feelings that belonged to them. This strategy, known as "repression" (that is pushing the knowledge of unbearable events and feelings out of awareness) is the major strategy that enables us as humans to survive very frightening experiences. Bowlby has written about this in great detail, showing how we develop a shutting-off process and the complicated variations of this we all engage in (1981). The important fact is, that no "shutting-off" is complete, and both the experiences and the processes continue to affect our behaviours for the rest of our lives. It is not just the events in themselves that then become so significant in our later years, but the fact that the *strategies* those early experiences determined go on being repeated so many times in different ways as the years go by. These tend to form very distinctive patterns of thinking, feeling, and behaving.

There seem to be two factors that make early painful attachment failures particularly significant in later life. One is that early experiences of loss tend to build up expectations of further losses, as well as difficulties in handling these when they come in reality. For the elderly, severe losses of all sorts are almost inevitable, so it seems a cruel fact that those who have had to struggle with losses very early in their lives are less likely to cope with the ones that come later. These losses come to us all when our parents die, as well as friends, colleagues, and, hardest of all for most people, the loss of partners. Our children, on becoming adult, often move long distances away, which can produce severe feelings of insecurity for some ageing parents. All these losses can reawaken the feelings associated with losses that occurred many years earlier. The second factor is that our memories change, so that earlier experiences often become more clear than they have ever been. As our current memories tend to weaken, so earlier memories become sharper and, in the process, painful memories that have been shut away often re-emerge, with all the sadness, regret, and feelings of blame and helplessness with which they were associated, tending to return in full measure. As an extreme example, one elderly woman in a retirement home became obsessed with memories of her experience of sexual abuse as a small girl. She was quite unable to explore it, or share it, in a helpful way in the state of mind that she was in at the time. This should have been done many years earlier. Instead, she had hidden the knowledge of it from everyone and in her old age became locked into the painful memories, repeating the experience of helplessness that she had had originally.

Ageist attitudes affecting psychotherapy

It is not surprising that both psychoanalysis and psychotherapy have been deeply influenced by the prevailing attitudes in our society, which is so strongly ageist that older people have not been deemed suitable for psychotherapy. This has some understandable aspects to it, as the very long-term thought patterns and behaviours that have come from early survival strategies can take a long time to alter and there may not be a "long time" left. But there is a more insidious reason that seems to be behind the reluctance to offer psychotherapy to older people. I believe that this has to do with the low valuing of the elderly in our society. Just as women have for generations been discounted in so many ways, so are elderly people today. Changes in society are occurring so fast, particularly in the fields of technology, that those who do not "keep up" are seen as "out of it" and, therefore, of less value. This is no new phenomenon! But as the speed of change increases, not only is there more and more to "catch up" with, but many of the values associated with previous times and ways of doing things, tend to be despised. E-mail is beginning to take over from letter writing, with the disparaging title of "snail mail" being given to letters, until the very concept of speed becomes valued above all else. This valuing of speed is intriguing, considering it has come at a time when we are living so much longer and, on the face of it, we have more time, not less!

Gender differences.

At this point it seems important to examine in greater detail how gender differences affect the experiences of ageing. Very recently, a plastic surgeon in Birmingham gave his view that older men are "like port wine" (implying that men ripen into something better as they age). Women, in contrast, he described as "like sour milk" (implying that women "go off", become something to be discarded as they grow older). Sadly, his view of elderly people is not uncommon, and this perception seems to play a large part in how differently elderly men are both perceived and treated, from elderly women. Germain Greer (1999, p. 231) describes today's society as being "more rotten with ageism than sexism". She writes of this as something that is now being experienced by many older people.

Women who have struggled all their lives with sexism are now experiencing an additional oppression due simply to growing older. It is very apparent that the sexist gap increases with age, largely due to the fact that older women are seen as no longer sexually attractive. It is quite commonplace for older men to leave partners of a similar age for much younger women. For older women to leave partners for younger men is rare, and when it happens they tend to be accused of "baby snatching", or suffer other such derogatory remarks. Masters and Johnson (1970) showed years ago that older women and younger men make a better match sexually than older men and younger women, because women's sexual capacities continue into old age. Men's inevitably diminish, yet the reality of this discrepancy always seems to be denied.

An even bigger discrepancy occurs in the roles that men and women play in public life. This has an equally lasting effect into their old age, even though there has been a small shift towards greater equality over the last fifty years. The four main areas where power is held, big business, law, politics and the academic world, are still very largely dominated by men. Their high positions often continue to be held until they are quite elderly. Women's status in these areas still tends to be due to their position as wives and this can be threatened, or even destroyed, if their husbands perceive their "progress" possibly being enhanced by having a younger woman as their partner. In the field of the media, there is an even more extreme variation of status, with many older men continuing to operate in films and on television while very few women do this. This is not due to women suddenly losing their acting abilities, but to the fact that older women are not considered attractive enough to be "on view". This perception seems to be held by many women as well as men, because they too are caught up in the prevailing sexist/ageist attitudes. There is no doubt that there have been some significant changes for the better over the last fifty years, but there is still a long way to go. If one accepts the basic view within Attachment Theory that experiences of severe or repeated emotional loss and deprivation lie at the heart of mental health problems, it requires us all to find the courage to challenge these fundamental imbalances in our society whenever we meet them, domestically, nationally, and internationally.

Perhaps the people who can undertake such challenges the most easily are those who have good enough views of their own sense of self, meaning that they do not have any wish to hold power over others in an oppressive way. As this chapter is concerning itself in particular with the experiences of older people, it seems the moment to look more closely at when and how we begin to get these "good enough" views of ourselves.

Appearances and their reflections

It is interesting that Bowlby, and other psychoanalysts before him, recognized how babies' sense of themselves comes, from the very beginning, through their mothers' or care-givers' face reflecting back a joyous and positive response to the baby's face. For most babies their smiles and gurgles get back an ecstatic response. This interaction, when it is positive, gives the baby a sense of happiness which is reflected back in an interchange of delight. For older people, especially older women, their wrinkled faces and grey hair produce a reflection that is the opposite of delight. They are perceived as no longer wanted or acceptable and their role is to become invisible. Macdonald (Macdonald & Rich, 1984) described vividly how, as she grew older and continued to go shopping with her lesbian partner, the shopkeepers invariably referred to her younger partner rather than to her. She found it a startling and unpleasant experience of exclusion.

Men, too, experience anxiety about their appearance as they age, and some face similar fears of being judged as "past it". Recently, I watched an older man who went into hospital for day surgery. He was facing the vulnerability most people feel prior to an operation. He chose to wear his university badge on his lapel and an army-type beret with his Air Force insignia upon it, as if he needed to state to the doctors and nurses that he was not "just a patient" but someone of status outside. This seems to say more about hospitals' attitudes to the elderly than it does about the patient.

Different feelings and experiences at the different stages of ageing

Not only are there very different individual experiences of ageing, but there is a huge difference between this experience for people in the fifty to sixty-five year age group and those in their seventies and eighties. Although the first group spans fifteen years, those within it share a lot of similar experiences. Some women hit a point of feeling they are "no longer young" on their fiftieth birthdays, with some experiencing quite severe anxieties about no longer being seen as sexually attractive. They start to worry excessively about their changing figures and the appearance of lines on their faces. It is probably impossible to know the exact amount of money spent in western society on various forms of plastic surgery, let alone on creams and potions, in an endeavour to maintain a more youthful look, though no doubt it runs into many millions of pounds. Men do not seem to be affected in the same way at this stage, as society still views them as "mature and interesting".

Perhaps, for women, this age is seen as a turning point because it tends to coincide with the menopause. This is an event that brings about a deep realization for women that they have moved to a different stage in life and so have "lost" the earlier one, because it ends the possibility of child bearing. No such "cut-off point" applies to men, some of whom are able to father children into their late seventies. It is important to recognize that while one woman may experience her menopause as a time of mourning a loss she feels she has not chosen, with all the sadness that involves, another may feel quite differently. There are some women who welcome their menopause. This seems particularly true for women who have had large families and feel relieved at the thought that there will be no further pregnancies. Others who feel equally relieved are those who have had very heavy periods over a number of years, have become anaemic and exhausted by them, and positively delight in their ending.

Over the last fifty years there have been good and wide-ranging changes for women in the field of sex. Now, they can to a large degree control their fertility with contraception, and if this fails or is not used, abortion is available albeit variably through the NHS. If women experience menstrual tension or menopausal symptoms they can discuss these openly with their doctor, and they are usually successfully treated with hormone replacement therapy or other remedies. It may be hard for young women today to appreciate just how punitive attitudes were over matters of sex and unwanted pregnancies even as recently as fifty years ago. One sad fact is that men in this age group seem to be reluctant to seek medical help. This has at last been recognized as a "problem", but there seems little certainty about how to change it, although efforts are being made to publicize the importance of seeking advice about worrying symptoms sooner rather than later.

Children leaving home

A quite different loss that is also an inevitable one for parents in this age group comes when children leave home. For some parents the so-called "empty nest" can be felt as an extremely difficult change to come to terms with. It is not only a loss of the parenting role within the home; it brings a replay of the original "two-some" for the parents. For parents who have remained close during the years they were bringing up their children, it can be experienced as offering more opportunities at last to do things together. For other parents, particularly those who have drifted apart and whose main point of communication has concerned the children, it can be a very stressful time. Fortunately, most children leave home in stages, so the sense of adjusting to it comes over a period of time. Occasionally, parents view with real relief the final departure of children that they have wished would leave home. Perhaps the worst scenario is when children have physically grown up, but have not done so psychologically, having been either so emotionally needed by their parents or so neglected by them that they have not been able to discover a separate sense of self, secure enough to manage the break of leaving home. This leaves such children so fearful of abandoning their parents, and feeling so lost without them, that they are unable to form close relations with other adults. Such people, most frequently men, can sometimes be stuck living with their ageing mothers, becoming extremely vulnerable at the time of their mother's death.

Loss of parents

The loss of parents is an anguish for most people, whatever kind of parenting they may have had. As with other major losses, how we are able to deal with it, depends on the relationship we have had with them and also the kind of attachments available to us at the time of the loss. When very warm and secure attachments have been continued through life with a parent, their death can feel less traumatic than when the attachment has been "insecure". It is as if the adult has a sense of grief because whatever was "wrong" or "missing" in the relationship with their parent can now never be "mended" or "put right". Mourning the loss of these parents can be very problematic.

One of the feelings so often expressed at the time of losing the second parent is the sense of "moving into the next generation" oneself. As one person put it, "*We* are now at the head of the line". For only children, this may be an extra hard loss to bear if they feel there is no one left who knew them as a child. Many people at this time find themselves full of memories and wanting to reminisce with others who remember their parents. Sometimes there are deep feelings of guilt in those who fear that they have not done enough to care for their parents, because their own lives have been so busy and demanding. Like every other major loss, reactions vary enormously. Some people feel "orphaned", whatever age they are when their parents die. Others have expressed a feeling that only on the death of their parents have they felt they were now finally grown up themselves.

Loss of adult children

This can happen at any time of course, but it seems particularly painful for parents when it occurs at the time of their offspring's middle years and their own much later ones. This may be partly because, these days, we do not expect our children to die before us, so it is a uniquely hard loss to bear. It ends all the parental hopes and dreams of how such a child would be in the future. The mourning tends to last a lifetime.

Retirement

During this period of fifty to sixty-five plus years, people are often overwhelmed by the number of new situations that all seem to be coming so close together. If the huge changes of parental loss and children leaving home coincide with retirement, or it follows soon after, it may feel as if too many changes, with the sense of loss that goes with them, are "all too much". Retirement, like all the other changes, can be experienced so differently by different people. Some large and responsible firms organize retirement plans for their staff in a very imaginative way. Others do nothing. One of the strangest aspects of it is the feeling that the day before one's sixty-fifth birthday one is perceived as capable of work, yet the next day one is not! With work being such a source of pressure for so many people today, and often working hours so long, a lot of people seek early retirement in the hope that they can then find part-time work somewhere else and so ease the complete and abrupt severing of their work life. For many men, retirement is harder to adjust to, than it is for women. This may not just be for the obvious reason that men's status and pay come largely from work, but that their lives are more dominated by it. Women tend to have far greater responsibilities towards the home and children, and often to friends and neighbours too, so that for them, parts of their life remain the same. Some men find retirement gives them a devastating loss of their sense of self, even if they have been grumbling for years about having to go to work.

For everyone who has to retire, there is some sense of having "dropped out of the world" as they fill in the word "retired" on a form that asks for their occupation. One of the hardest aspects for many people is the loss of income and for some, particularly women, a very low level of pension. There are some concessions that help, for example transport, discounts at many places of interest with opportunities for leisure pursuits, and learning of all kinds. Older people have set up many organizations for themselves, such as "The University of the Third Age" and "Growing Old Disgracefully" (for women), among others. Grandparenting can be experienced as wonderfully rewarding. For some it becomes a full-time role, though this is changing, as many older people freed from parenting their own children are apparently more reluctant to give up any work that they may be doing to take it all on again. Whatever the retirement scene may hold in the way of feelings of loss, what seems most important is to perceive it as one of challenge and opportunity. New things can be done for which there was never previously sufficient time.

Loss of partner, colleagues and friends

The loss of a life-long partner, whether married or not, is probably the biggest loss in life for most people. When it happens in the later stages of life, to those who are in their seventies or eighties, it can be experienced as a devastating blow, even when expected. It can feel like a "little death" of their own, as someone put it to me. The words "wife" and "husband" define us in terms of beings attached to someone else. "Widow" and "widower" are words defining loss and non-attachment. In addition, the word "widow" carries some very distressful associations that are not linked with widower: "widow's weeds" and "widow's mite" imply someone very low in the order of things. A very hard loss can be felt by a same-sex partner, for whom we have no name. For such a person there is often fear that their loss will not be recognized sufficiently for what it is. In some instances the relationship was kept hidden, so the loss cannot even be shared.

At this time, family and friends are needed to support the partner through the grieving process and to help them find new ways of living, yet sadly at this stage many elderly people have lost their closest or oldest friends. It seems that consoling the bereaved is becoming more and more perceived as a role for professionals, with bereavement counsellors called in, particularly when there is a disaster entailing loss of life. Perhaps in some ways this is a good thing, as it gives recognition to the shock and severity of such losses. I wonder though, whether it also betrays the fact that everyone is so busy and too afraid of commitment to offer what is needed as an attachment figure—being available and responsive. So many people, instead, feel embarrassed. They don't know what to say and cross the road to the other side if they see a person who has recently been bereaved coming along. Will the time ever come when people in this nation are sufficiently "emotionally literate", to use Susie Orbach's phrase (1994), to feel confident and natural in responding to others' emotional needs, not only at a day to day level but also at times of crisis?

Commonest fears

The commonest fears among elderly people concern what will happen to them if they become seriously ill, can no longer cope at home, have partners who need caring for in ways that can no longer be managed and, above all, how they will cope with being moved into residential care. All these fears are not without foundation, for residential caring for the elderly in our society is, with some wonderful exceptions, at a very seriously low level. Inside this generalized fear of loss of independence is the worst fear of losing choice, of having no "say" in their lives. Many care homes are closing because they are not profitable enough for their owners. Those run by local authorities have huge problems with under-staffing, under-qualified staff, and a rapid staff turnover. Fees go up to unaffordable levels, and case conferences are held to which the person concerned is not invited. Arber and Ginn (1991) write movingly about experiences in residential care, especially how it affects women. The very way such "care" is organized denies the attachment needs of the elderly. This is demonstrated at a very simple level, by how lounge chairs are placed in a circle round the room, thus making close talk impossible. Women are much more likely to be admitted to residential care than men, by the fact that men, having a shorter life expectancy, tend to die first. As a consequence of this, women are more likely to be left alone, and have far less chance of finding a new partner. Men in residential homes seem to be rarities. There seems little chance of matters improving. If the attachment needs of the elderly are even to be recognized, yet alone met in our society, the training and pay for carers of the elderly need to be raised so that it properly equates with the value of their work. At present it remains abysmally low, reflecting how little it is currently valued.

Lack of affordable housing is now a serious matter in this country. It is of great concern to elderly people, who often have enormous fear that they will not be able to keep up their homes or get help to do so. For many elderly people their homes hold strong attachment histories, of long-gone parents, or more recent memories of children or partners. There seems to be little recognition of the traumatic effect on elderly people of moving. Many stay on in houses too big for them for this reason, as well as the fear of the upheaval of a move. They may also want to keep rooms available for children and grandchildren to visit, even though this may occur only occasionally.

There is a huge need now for a radical new way for these

problems to be tackled at government or local authority level. Specially designed cooperative housing schemes need to be set up for the elderly. They should be built on brown sites, with easy access to shops and transport. Elderly people in their sixties could be encouraged to sell their houses when they are occupied by only one or two people. They could then be used for families or converted into flats. Elderly couples or single elderly people could then buy into cooperative schemes, living in small houses or flats on a site with communal areas providing a variety of facilities. Some nursing care in a separate wing would also be an essential feature, not limited to terminal care. The residents would move around within the site according to their needs, and not be made to leave unless they needed hospital treatment. They could return to the site for nursing care afterwards and this would free many hospital beds. Communities like this operate successfully in other countries, such as Holland. The most important features must be that the residents play a role in running them, that places are available for families to stay for short visits, and some type of insurance payments are made to cover unexpected extra costs e.g., for nursing help. Such sites would not become "ghettos " for the elderly, because part of the scheme would be to open some of the site's communal areas to the community around it for the use of a variety of clubs and groups.

In the 1970s I produced a detailed scheme for the housing needs of the elderly, hoping to gain from it myself! The response at the time from many friends and neighbours with whom I shared it was that "old age" for them, seemed too far away to think about. This attitude seemed to endorse how good we are at avoiding thinking about situations that we prefer not to face. It seems now increasingly urgent that as a nation we address a number of social problems that are arising as the proportion of elderly people in the population is increasing so rapidly. Between 1951 and 2001 the proportion of the population over the age of sixty has risen from 16% to 21%, but perhaps even more startling is the increase in the number of over eighty-fives. In 1951 there were 0.2 million and at the last census in 2001 there were 1.1 million, according to The National Statistics Office. This suggests that there could be an important role for the "young old" to play in helping to care for the "old old", in the knowledge that in doing so, they will have care in their turn if it is needed. Schemes like the one described would provide security, help to end loneliness, and provide an invaluable purpose in their lives for many elderly people. They could become enriched through contributing to such schemes, which could become interestingly varied according to local needs.

Facing death

At the core of attitudes to ageing and the many fears surrounding it is the fact that it is the phase of life that will lead to death. It has always been said that we humans are incapable of envisioning our own death. I am not sure that this is true, but however we may view it, there is no doubt that our religious views will profoundly affect how we feel. For those who deeply believe there is some form of life after death, there is hope of renewing attachments in some form with those who have died before them. For others who hold no such beliefs, there is a profoundly important need to be able to express their desire either to detach themselves, if that is what they wish, or, the opposite, to be with people whom they love and know care about them as their life ends. The saddest situations arise when the dying will not discuss their needs and thoughts for fear of upsetting their family and friends and, in turn, the family members will behave in the same way for fear of upsetting their dying relative. Unless they give very clear signals to the contrary, most people want to know if their death is near, so that they can say things that perhaps they have not felt able to before, or make important decisions, or to let special wishes be known. Perhaps of all our institutions, hospices have the best ethos for comprehending attachment needs. In 1999, Dr Murray Parkes commented to me that whereas earlier hospice care concentrated on lessening patients' pain, this has been so successfully dealt with that priority can now be given to offering emotional support through counselling to patients and their relatives.

Conclusions

The most important point in this chapter to iterate in conclusion is the vital need for our society to change its attitude to the elderly.

There are signs that the importance of the attachment needs of the young are beginning to be recognized, but this is not so for the elderly. Some older people who have had secure attachments in their early life and whose attachment figures in their later life continue to be responsive to them, may well live a fulfilling and contented life to the end, especially if they also have reasonable health and an acceptable income. Sadly, others whose attachment needs have been denied or neglected, whose health may be poor and with inadequate incomes, often lead very isolated, lonely lives, with high levels of depression and anxiety.

There is no organization in this country equivalent to "grey power" in the USA, but it is time that older people in this country "came out", not whinging, nor demanding, but rather making their proper needs known wherever and whenever they can, enlisting advocates if necessary to help them do so. Only in this way will new policies be made, so that elderly people may experience their later years as a time of change rather than decline and, most importantly, find it is a time when new attachments can be made. These would not deny the lessening of physical abilities, but could occur in spite of them. In the process, we may explode some of the myths about ageing that still seem so strongly to influence the way elderly people, particularly women, are both perceived and treated in our society and, too often, how they perceive themselves.

CHAPTER FIVE

Attachment and social policy

Peter Marris

Introduction

F rom birth, children are ready to begin the relationship which, more than any other, will form their personalities. Within their first year, unless they are very unlucky, they become uniquely attached to their primary care-givers—mother, especially, father or grandmother, or their adoptive parents. As they grow, and the attachment evolves, so their confidence grows with it. They begin to explore the social world that attachment opens to them, and they learn to trust or mistrust it, as they have learned to trust or mistrust the attachment itself. So this first relationship to our parenting figures profoundly influences who we grow up to be, and how we see the world we make for ourselves. Secure and nurturing childhoods foster adults who, whatever their difficulties, have an inner confidence to withstand the misfortunes of life, and an ability to love and trust. Insecurity fosters mistrust, self-contempt, loneliness, hatred, and revenge. All too often, those whose yearning for attachment has been abused or neglected in their childhood inflict the same cruelty on their own children.

You would think, then, that every society would do its utmost to

71

protect and support a relationship so fundamental to our well-being. It would do all it could to give mothers and fathers the time and energy they need to bond with their children. It would encourage parental leave and flexible employment schedules. It would try to prevent changes that disrupt families and the networks of kinship and mutual support on which they depend. And it would try to ensure that every family was guaranteed basic economic security. Yet the ideas which guide the policies of modern nations contradict these simple and seemingly obvious prescriptions in almost every way. In this chapter, I will try to explain how and why this is so, and how, instead, we could use our understanding of attachment to change them.

Part of the problem lies with the way the theory of attachment has been misunderstood. Its profound implications for human development were partly obscured by the circumstances in which John Bowlby, the psychologist whose life work was to develop the theory of Attachment, first put his ideas forward.

The feminist attack on Bowlby's Theory of Attachment

As my study of theory progressed, it was gradually borne in upon me that the field I had set out to plough so lightheartedly was no less than the one that Freud had started tilling sixty years earlier, and that it contained all those same rocky excrescences and thorny entanglements that he had encountered and grappled with—love and hate, anxiety and defence, Attachment and loss. What had deceived me was that my furrows had been started from a corner diametrically opposite to the one at which Freud had entered and through which analysts have always followed. [Bowlby, 1982, p. xi]

Bowlby's "corner" was a request from the World Health Organization to advise on the mental health of homeless children, and how best to safeguard the health of children separated from their mothers.

In the first part of the report, I presented evidence and formulated a principle: "What is believed to be essential for mental health is that the infant and young child should experience a warm, intimate and continuous relationship with his mother (or permanent mother substitute) in which both find satisfaction and enjoyment". [ibid., p. xi]

So, from the outset, Attachment Theory evolved around social policy, as a search to understand the qualities and conditions of healthy attachments, and how these qualities, or the lack of them, affected a child's development. Such an inquiry led to the circumstances in which parents raised their children—their jobs, earnings, and childcare arrangements; divorce, separation, and bereavement.

The findings of the early research, since they emphasized how hurtful separation from mother could be, even for a short while, seemed to imply that mothers of young children should stay home and nurture them. By the 1970s, advocates of women's rights were insisting on a wife's right to a career equal to her husband's, and two incomes were needed more and more to meet household expenses. So Attachment Theory came to be challenged as both reactionary and cruel. It was reactionary, because it implied a return to a traditional domestic role for women, and cruel because it made mothers feel guilty about going out to work to earn a living when they had no choice. The controversy entangled Attachment Theory in an argument about whether institutionalized childcare was good or bad for young children. In the context of British social policy, Attachment Theory seemed to have little to offer except a traditional ideal of mothering that was no longer realizable or even desired. Its crucial insights were distorted and misunderstood.

But the stay-at-home mother is a very recent, middle-class ideal. In nearly every society, throughout history, mothers have been farmers, weavers, pottery makers, midwives, healers, wage earners, as well as the caretakers of their children. The home bound mother, devoting herself to her domestic tasks, is a Victorian invention—an ideal of gender roles where motherhood and purity were set against the harsh, competitive, and polluted world of industrial enterprise. Whether the bond between a child and her or his parents is reliable and nurturing, or fragile and hurtful, depends on a complex of social arrangements, which vary from society to society but everywhere include not only the immediate family, but also the kin group and the community. The crucial question is not whether a mother should stay at home or go out to work, but whether her society supports her, so that, at home or out to work, her children feel securely attached. And this is a much larger question of how resources and roles are allocated in society. It concerns men as much as women; the rights and obligations of employer and employee;

the way work is organized; wages and the forms of social insurance. All these arrangements are influenced by the way a society regards, or disregards, attachment and how well it supports the whole range of relationships in which bonds of attachment can flourish.

Attachment and meaning

The Theory of Attachment sets out four principles that together largely define the circumstances in which people can fulfil the potential of their lives. The bond between a child and his or her parenting figures is crucial to the child's development, and this bond, once formed, is a unique relationship; no other care-giver, however loving, can substitute for these primary attachment figures (although insecure attachments can be modified through other secure attachments, or with therapeutic interventions). As children grow up, they form adult attachments—typically to a sexual partner, and sometimes to a community, or an idealized leader— which share the uniqueness and emotional intensity of the parent– child bond. Last, these attachments underlie our purposes, and largely constitute the meaning of our lives. Ideally, then, the institutions of society should enable its members to nurture and sustain secure, benign attachments, both in childhood and adult life. Conversely, a society where its members are confident of being loved, and able to form loving relationships, is likely to create such institutions.

The attachment of a child to its parents is the primary relationship through which we learn to become social beings. Since our welfare depends upon securing the protection of our attachment figures, the relationship is our central concern throughout childhood, and its unresolved insecurities linger into adult life. Through this interaction between parent and child, each learns a set of strategies by which to manage the relationship. Even within the first few months, an infant's behaviour begins to be informed by learning, so that long before a boy or girl can express meaning in words, each has already established a powerful organization of emotions, desires, and patterns of experience centred upon the two essential tasks of childhood. These two tasks are to secure the attention of attachment figures and to learn to use growing abilities.

A young child has to figure out, above all, how to get what is needed from attachment figures—including the need not to be interfered with when trying to learn some new skill, without ever being abandoned to the consequences of failure.

Since the attachment relationship is the source of virtually all security, comfort, and nourishment in early life, the management of attachment is the starting point for understanding every other kind of relationship. How a child learns to handle it will provide that child's basic assumptions about order, control, trust, self-protection, and self-worth. Since his or her coping strategies will evolve out of these assumptions, each new experience is likely to both confirm and modify them. From this a sense of identity will gradually mature—a sense of who one is in the world, and what kind of world it is grounded in the experiences of childhood. It is made up of an intricate set of assumptions about the social groups to which one belongs, the rights and obligations entailed thereby, and how conflicts between incompatible loyalties are to be resolved.

Our experience of attachment, therefore, largely determines where we will turn for both material and emotional support. The social groups with which we identify admit us to communities of mutual help, from which we may gain respect, collective pride, and a sense of being part of a more enduring, powerful human presence than a single life can accomplish. A kin group, a gang, a profession, a political movement, a nation, or religion is typical of such communities and they convey, as well as rights and obligations, a history. Even if such identities are sometimes burdensome, we cannot live without them, and we can only sometimes choose which to live with. They provide the membership through which each of us can create a sufficiently stable and predictable set of relationships to cope with the world around us and achieve our purposes. They define what others expect from us, what their behaviour should mean, how we should respond, what we can reasonably hope for, and why it all makes sense as a meaningful way of living. Even when we have to make moral choices in isolation, we have in mind not just our conscience, but also an imagined community that will affirm our integrity, drawn from our experience of those who have loved and respected us.

The meaning we make of our lives, therefore, is embedded in the history of our attachments, and the histories of the communities in which those attachments were fostered. Our sense of it, at any particular moment, depends on how we use those histories to confront the present and the future. It is a subtle, intricate structure of organization, never finished nor wholly consistent, constantly adapting and assimilating. It is both unique to each individual and responsive to events that affect its crucial relationships. Under the stress of unemployment, migration, cultural innovation, and social conflict, both the internal and external organization of meaning is likely to be threatened. How it resists these threats will depend in part on its internal structure, and in part on the structure of external pressures. It may become more rigid and defensive, or enrich itself by creative assimilation. But it is not infinitely adaptable, and its disintegration is the worst misfortune that can befall us, since it robs us of any reason to live.

Attachment and the development

Now compare this account of human well-being with the idea of well-being which dominates most national and international policies. Both national governments and international agencies like the World Bank tend to equate insecurity and despair with poverty. Certainly, lacking the necessities of life threatens every aspect of well-being. But this single-minded emphasis on ending poverty means, first of all, that the less material aspects of well-being tend to be forgotten. More dangerously, it leads to an uncritical acceptance of economic growth, as the only way to reduce poverty. And economic growth, almost every government believes, depends on promoting competitive capitalism throughout the world as quickly as possible. But global capitalism can be profoundly disruptive of the kinds of relationship of attachment and community on which our sense of the meaning of our lives depends.

Anti-poverty policies are concerned primarily with biological well-being—with food, water, shelter, health care—and in so far as they address psychological needs, they are concerned mostly with education, as the learning of instrumental skills enables those who have been excluded from employment to qualify for jobs. These needs are certainly crucial, but they have in common a characteristic that they do not share with the conditions for our mental well-being.

They can all be met by interchangeable units of consumption. That is, one nourishing meal is equivalent to another; one competent teacher is as effective as another; any properly trained doctor can treat a common illness.

This interchangeability is central to the logic of markets: prices are set by quantifying supply and demand, and this would be impossible unless the good in question is reproducible. Confronted with less tangible, psychological needs, market-centred policies can only try to reduce them to the equivalent of a good—as units of utility or happiness, and, therefore, once again something that can be quantified and interchanged. The same utilitarianism underlies the ideals of the welfare state. As a contract between each member of society and the state, guaranteeing at least a minimal protection against hardship, it recognizes only the loss of material well-being, which can be quantified in the payment of a benefit. It provides no protection against the loss of meaning, of identity and self-worth that accompany unemployment, separation, or the decay of a once vital community.

The relationships which matter most to us are not interchangeable or readily transferable. Children attach themselves to their own, unique parents, not to a generic source of parenting skills. The people we love are unique individuals. If we lose them, we grieve for them; we do not turn to a substitute. Grief itself, especially when we are bereft of someone very close to us, is a long, painful, at times despairing, search to recover faith in the meaning of life. Hence the conditions that support the well-being of our mental organization are fundamentally different from those that can support our biological organization.

Ideally, children should grow up in a family where their crucial attachments are secure—stable and intact throughout the length of their childhood. And that family should be supported by a network of relationships of which it is part, through which mutual help and mutual respect are exchanged, and shared values affirmed—a kinship group, the congregation of a church, a trade union, a circle of friends. Most people anywhere in the world would, I think, recognize and endorse this basic prescription for a nurturing society. Not that every family or community is benign. But unloving parenting, or the punitiveness of insecure communities, are not arguments against attachment and belonging. They show, rather, how deeply both individuals and societies can be damaged when the impulse for attachment is rejected or repressively manipulated.

This implies the need to support and maintain the crucial specific, unique, nurturing and mutually affirming relationships over long periods of time. It is in such relationships that we characteristically speak of love; and the love of someone or something, love for its own sake, as an attachment that requires no other justification, is surely the most universal and powerful source of meaning. Attachment implies a relationship to that particular, irreplaceable individual whom we love. If we try to reinterpret such attachments in terms of generalizable, theoretically marketable goods—for instance, as a need to nurture and be nurtured—we miss their essential quality. Mothering and fathering become childcare. Not that childcare is undesirable, but it has a different meaning. So it is impossible, and misguided, to try to subsume these relationships under some cost–benefit analysis of supply and demand.

Competition and the burdens of uncertainty

By contrast, competitive capitalism promotes an ideal of minimal commitment. In an uncertain world of constantly evolving markets and products, the goal of the successful firm is to accept the fewest possible long-term obligations, especially to its workers, and to shrink the size of its core organization to the smallest possible constant. In this way, it maximizes its chances of survival, is nimble enough to switch products, relocate its production, dismiss workers in one place to exploit the potential of a cheaper labour force elsewhere, shuffle its management, and open new markets.

At the same time, while the managers of a firm try to maximize their freedom of manoeuvre, they must also try to limit the freedom of those on whom they depend. Freedom of choice is only of value if you can predict what the consequences of your choice will be. So you need to secure commitments that, if you decide on such and such an action, a promised response will follow. And if you are powerful enough, you can secure that commitment without making any commitment of your own in return. So, for instance, if a large corporation is considering whether to locate in a certain city, it will demand assurances that a compliant government will be ready and eager to provide the tax incentives and planning clearances it desires, help to recruit the workers, suppress disruptive militancy, and provide the necessary education. It wants assurances that the land it needs will be made available at an acceptable price, and that workers with the skills it requires are ready to be hired. But the firm will seek to avoid any reciprocal commitment that might constrain its future action. This increases the uncertainty for everyone else.

Again and again, in the hope of gaining jobs and economic growth, cities and nations grant concessions and undertake policies, only to see the firms they sought to attract go elsewhere, or abandon them after a few years. This makes it increasingly difficult to build the kind of economies, locally or nationally, that offer stable employment. Without stable employment, communities lose their coherence, as people are constantly forced to move and readjust. Networks of mutual support wither and die. Grandparents are separated from grandchildren. Parents are under greater stress, and their children will suffer.

The poor suffer most. The logic of competitive advantage in an uncertain world implies that we all use whatever control we have over relationships to constrain the freedom of action of others on whom we depend, while protecting our own freedom. Powerful firms insulate themselves from the fluctuation of the market by subcontracting production, at the same time ridding themselves of any social responsibility for the conditions their subcontractors impose. As this strategy plays itself out down the hierarchy of power, the greatest burden of uncertainty falls on the weakest, who are left with few choices, and even fewer assurances of their future. They are likely to end up in insecure jobs, working for insecure firms, to whom other more powerful firms subcontract their production. And these marginal workers are likely also to live in the most marginal environments—the shanty towns on unstable slopes or dangerous flood plains for which government accepts little responsibility, and where even the most essential needs can only tenuously be improvised.

So there is a contradiction at the heart of the way governments and international agencies seek to end poverty. They take it for granted that ending poverty depends on economic growth. And the only effective strategy of growth, prevailing economic theory teaches, is through world-wide, open, competitive markets. But as the most powerful actors—banks and corporations and trading nations—manoeuvre to protect their interests amid the uncertainties of this global competition, they shift a growing burden of uncertainty on to those who are weaker. This burden of uncertainty undermines the conditions in which secure attachments and stable communities can flourish. So those who economic growth was supposed to help, suffer, and their children suffer, as their attachments are disrupted by forced migration, fickle employment opportunities, loss of traditional markets, fragmented social supports, and alienation from their roots. Statistics may show that average national income per head is going up, but the relationships on which the quality of life depends are being pulled apart.

Apologists may argue that competitive capitalism will, by ending poverty, eventually create the basis of universal security. But such an argument fundamentally misunderstands the nature of security. To meet everyone's material needs while destroying the basis of their psychological needs is a prescription for universal despair. Even in countries with high per capita incomes and low rates of unemployment, the inability to sustain stable, long-term relationships impoverishes the meaning of life. And the malaise of insecurity can only intensify, as the logic of global economic competition plays itself out. When trillions of dollars wash around the world each day, and an economic crisis in Thailand can at once destabilize the economy of Brazil; when transnational corporations manoeuvring to maintain their competitive advantage are richer than most nations, the potential for social disruption is amplified to a scale we can barely grasp.

Things fall apart

The greater the insecurity of our vital relationships, the harder it becomes to put our trust in them. Anxiety gives way to apathy and despair and, in reaction, people will begin to look for comfort and a sense of meaning in forms of belonging which seem invulnerable to the uncertainties of everyday life. Rigid religions, for instance, which promise eternal bliss in an afterlife, whatever the misfortunes of the present, create both certainty and a community of fellow believers. The sense of identity and worth they offer is an idealized abstraction that no experience can impugn. They demand absolute and unquestioning adherence. The harder it becomes to make sense of life, the more people will be drawn to such mythological, other-worldly religions, which seem to offer an escape from all the bewildering uncertainties of their present circumstances. So, for instance, the orphaned Afghan refugees of decades of civil war grasp at the redemptive meaning of a messianic, puritan Islam, which holds out the promise of a gloriously rewarded martyrdom. But that other-worldliness also renders them impotent, except to justify acts of wholesale repudiation and destruction. As Yugoslavia fell apart, young people who had never before thought of themselves as Serbs or Bosnians, Muslims or orthodox Christians, began to snatch at idealized ethnic identities, in search of something to belong to in a disintegrating world. Religion and ethnicity can both readily be manipulated into violent conflict when the frustrations of everyday life become unbearable.

So economic growth, when it disrupts communities and pulls apart attachments, risks foundering under the rage, frustration, apathy, and despair it provokes. This is not an argument against the need to create the resources to feed, shelter, educate, and take care of the good health of everyone in the world; nor is one positing that markets cannot help to achieve this. My point is rather that relationships of attachment are as fundamentally important to our well-being as relationships of production, and neither can be subsumed under the other. Attachment cannot be conceived in terms of marketable goods, any more than markets can be conceived in terms of attachments. We have to recognize that the conditions that sustain secure attachments are often in conflict with the ideal conditions of market efficiency.

Reconciling attachment and growth

Once we confront these incompatibilities we can begin to think how to reconcile them. Farming on small scattered plots may preclude the growing of higher-yielding seeds or valuable cash crops, but it supports a way of life embedded in a network of social reciprocity, which land consolidation destroys. Abolishing tariffs may give people access to better quality goods at lower prices, but it may destroy the communities which depended on protected markets. Whenever resources are reallocated, the relationships in which they had been embedded wither, and the repercussions of that loss may spread throughout society. Once this is acknowledged, other strategies of growth begin to emerge—cooperatives through which very small scale farmers can market crops; microlending; new technologies adapted to the conditions of an emerging market. Maintaining public services may seem more expensive than contracting them out to private companies, but that calculation ignores the social cost of ending secure, reliable, public employment.

But do we always have to trade off social stability for growth, and growth for stability? Just to recognize that we have such a choice is some progress, especially if we acknowledge that those who benefit from the growth and those who suffer from the social disruption are often not the same. But beyond that, cooperation and social reciprocity may have more economic advantages than the logic of competitive capitalism implies.

In the face of uncertainty, as I have described, a simple calculation suggests that the winning strategy maximizes one's own freedom of action while constraining others and minimizing commitments. And as everyone tries to manoeuvre in this way, as best they can, an ever more crushing burden of uncertainty is passed down from stronger to weaker, until it rests most heavily on those with the fewest resources. But the effect of this is to create a world in which all relationships are increasingly unpredictable, as everyone is forced to play the same game. If employers seeks to minimize commitment to their employees, the employees will in turn have no loyalty to them; if corporations refuse to accept obligations to the nations which court them, those nations have little incentive to honour commitments they have been forced to make; and if no one is making any commitment to the fifth of the world's population living in desperate poverty, that fifth has little to lose by turning against the rest of us.

The logic of competitive control eventually undermines the predictability of all relationships, maximizing uncertainty. But the greater the uncertainties, the higher the economic cost of investment, because the risk of failure from all manner of social causes increases. Long-term planning is inhibited, otherwise promising opportunities are rejected, banks become more cautious, insurance

costs are higher. So, perversely, unconstrained competition ov\
distribution of resources ends by creating fewer resourc\
distribute. There is, therefore, a powerful argument that reciprocity
and commitment are, after all, in the interests of the powerful as
well as the weak. Though they inhibit freedom of action in the
immediate future, they make the longer-term future more predictable, extending the range of both investment and research. The
single-minded, unconditional advocacy of competitive markets
would lead ultimately to such disintegrated societies that no
markets could flourish.

Because economic knowledge is assertively theorized and
intellectually prestigious, we have tended to assume that the
prescriptions of economics are unassailable. There are no Nobel
prizes for psychological understanding. The value of love and self-
worth, of a sense of belonging, is acknowledged in principle and
then forgotten or dismissed, because it is not quantifiable; it is
"soft" or fuzzy, even sentimental, unlike the "hard" facts of
quantitative analysis. But we almost certainly understand more
about attachment than we do about growth, since we have lived in
families and social groups for thousands of years, while the
economic theory that both justifies and explains the processes of
industrial capitalism is a creation of the last two centuries.
Attachment Theory is at least as rigorous, as grounded in empirical
research, and as universally relevant as anything that economics can
offer. If we acknowledge it and use it, we can channel economic
growth into institutions that reinforce, instead of undermine, the
bonds of attachment that make life worth living.

CHAPTER SIX

Torture, political violence and attachment

Jeremy Woodcock

Introduction

I n this chapter we seek to understand the impact of torture and organized political violence on ordinary people and see how violence that is overwhelming affects people's emotional attachments. In reaching an understanding of how violence may fundamentally alter survivors' emotional attachments, we need to learn that torture and political violence do not happen in isolation. They are part of a wider global political picture and many people who are survivors of political violence fly into exile and become refugees in order to escape with their lives. The result of this is that attachments are not only altered by violence but also are fundamentally changed in very practical ways by separation and loss.

War, political atrocity and vulnerability

Since the end of the Second World War and the formation of the United Nations it is staggering to realize that there have been over

170 wars in which well over 30 million people are estimated to have died, and the greatest number of those have been civilian deaths. Political regimes have used violence to enforce their rule and most often community leaders and other prominent people, such as teachers, doctors, religious leaders, and local politicians have been made the target of oppression. This is because oppressive regimes and political movements realize that if local leadership is broken, resistance to them will be harder to organize and maintain. Often, whole groups and communities have been subjected to violence. Social networks, neighbourhoods, whole family groups, people's histories, and whole ways of life have been destroyed deliberately and indiscriminately. This often happens because regimes characterize the "enemy" as less than human. In doing this they weaken the fundamental resistance in themselves and their soldiers to killing the innocent.

People's proximity to political events will shape how they suffer and survive, but this can take different forms. For instance, some people may feel strong because they are part of the resistance to oppression. Others may feel like weak and unlucky victims of politics; this is particularly true of people swept up into genocide, where whole populations are persecuted such as the Armenian people in Turkey in the 1920s, the European Jews in the 1930s and, more recently, the Tutsi people in Rwanda, Bosnian Muslims during the war in former Yugoslavia, and communities in Indonesia, Afghanistan, and Iraq.

People caught up in political violence always ask the question, "Why me?" This happens not least because torture and organized state violence do not only happen to magnificent brave people but forces its way into ordinary life, and ordinary relationships. What frequently happens is that torture and violence get into people's bodies and minds in powerful and unwanted ways. So, there's the father who cannot share with his eleven-year-old son the terror that happened to him in prison, although the son knows instinctively what happened. Then there's the woman who guiltily realizes that a gulf has opened up between herself and her husband, because she was raped as a form of torture. Then, too, what of the lad who is imprisoned and tortured just because he is old enough to carry a gun and might one day become a threat to the regime. And the African woman escaping from political violence who had to leave her two daughters at the border because there wasn't enough money for them all to escape together? All of them quite rightly ask, "Why me?" "Why us?" For recovery from the violence of torture and oppression to occur, that vital question needs some sort of answer.

The question will always have a complicated answer that involves politics and society in addition to personal matters. For it is not only physical and emotional attachments that are broken by political violence, but also the basic belief in a trustworthy world. This belief is one of the primary qualities that develops through secure emotional attachment, and it is fundamentally challenged by violence.

Surviving the trauma of political violence

People's reactions to severe hardship are very different; it must not be assumed that every survivor of war and torture will be traumatized and in need of emotional help. Survivors of torture can be very hardy, especially if they have reasonable self-esteem, secure relationships and opportunities to mix with other people and make meaningful connections with them. Also, if they can hold on to a well balanced sense of control, enjoy some success and achievement, maintain the ability to reflect on what has happened to them, and make sense of things in a meaningful way, then they are more likely to have the resilience to help them withstand their pain and make it possible for them to assimilate their experience. With these qualities and opportunities, recovery from torture, violence, and atrocity can be a gradual but sure thing.

People are most vulnerable when they are isolated because their families and loved ones are not available. That is, people are most at risk when attachments are broken in a very real way because family members have been killed or left behind in the struggle to escape. Very often survivors will be in a state of shock, grief, and bereavement because of the murder of family and friends, which they may have witnessed. They will also have lost all the ordinary but valuable things about the culture and neighbourhood where they grew up.

Loss may be especially sharp when people flee into exile. This may seem ironic if we assume that war and torture are now at a "safe distance". However, by escaping into exile, refugees lose a great deal of what makes life meaningful in an ordinary, everyday sort of way. As one magnificently courageous African women said, "I am so thankful to have escaped with my life, but in exile the food is as tasteless as if it were cooked without salt." Then, too, refugees escaping from political violence will also be vulnerable when the society where they seek asylum is hostile and rejecting. This is happening more and more in the West.

One of the problems of exile is that, by definition, the condition is ambiguous and open-ended. For the resourceful it can be an opportunity. For the devastated it can feel overwhelmingly insecure because the expected pathways through life have totally changed. Even so, refugees are not passive victims; they cooperate and reach personal deals with themselves and with the host society. For instance, Chilean refugees in the USA often characterized exile as like "being in the belly of the beast" because they blamed the USA for its involvement in the overthrow of the left-wing Chilean government and the political violence which forced them into exile. They emphasized the need to stick together and live cooperatively but as time passed some took advantage of the commercial opportunities that life in the USA offered. As they did so, the community had to revise their relations with each other and with those in their new home in ways that were more "elastic". This allowed members of the community to thrive in the new society without appearing to betray the basic belief in the community and its values (Eastmond, 1997). These adjustments can be seen, for example, in the stories that exiled communities come to write about how things were "then" and how they are now.

Torture, terror and loss

Torture brings those lucky enough to survive literally close to death. They will have experienced the sense that they are expendable; that their life hung on a thread; that someone else, not them, had ultimate control over whether they lived or died, had food or water, even when they could use the toilet. Those near-death experiences can cause a disastrous weakening of their inner strength, as if the inside of their head and body have been taken over. Torture invades survivors with incredible intensity. They find themselves thinking over and over again about what has happened. They have flashbacks in which they relive what has occurred. As they drop off to sleep and relax they have vivid recollections of things. During sleep they have dreams and nightmares that replay the violence they have suffered. Often the only way to manage such strong recollections and feelings is to dissociate, which actually means to "tune out" or "switch off", to be distracted, or to temporarily go "into another world".

The obvious truth is that refugees are persecuted by outside forces, but the consequence of that experience for them is that they actually feel persecuted inside. They are deeply ashamed of what has happened to them, and this is particularly true of women and men who are raped. They may also feel humiliated because they have not been able to protect family, friends and, in particular, children, from violence. They may also feel weakened and humiliated because they were in such intense fear that they became incapable under torture. Very often they will feel full of regret and sadness about everything they have lost, wishing intensely that things could be different.

The downward social changes of life in exile add to the impact on the survivor's inner experience of weakness and loss of control over their life. For one thing, there is loss of status. One comes across highly qualified people whose qualifications mean nothing to the host society, who have to start again at the bottom. There are also community leaders with no community to lead. Then, too, losses of material possessions are huge; people who once lived well, are now scraping together a life in a bed-sitting room. Sometimes survivors feel too broken, downhearted, irritable, or distracted to play an effective part in family life, and this makes the impact of torture doubly cruel.

Torture and attachment

What we have seen is that torture and exile sever many fundamental emotional attachments in people's lives: attachment to country; to neighbours and colleagues; to parents, children, wider family, relatives, and friends. We will now go on to consider how torture affects attachment in a more basic, psychological way.

Attachment Theory explains how parents tend to pass on to their children the quality of attachment they experienced themselves as children. It suggests that parents with good quality attachments naturally tend to pass those qualities on to their children, whereas children with difficult attachments often seem to have parents who had muddled and difficult attachments themselves.

As we have argued throughout this book, Attachment Theory claims that we need emotional security in order to develop and thrive, and we seek it with those we love. John Bowlby, one of the original creators of Attachment Theory, observed that when we are most upset, frightened, and stressed, we seek out the person to whom we are most emotionally attached (Bowlby, 1988). An understanding of this drive towards attachment when we feel most vulnerable, can help us to understand why the violence, separation, and loss that torture survivors and refugees typically experience can have a particularly devastating effect on their emotions, and why political violence is so deeply shocking, lonely, and a source of psychological trauma.

We can perhaps understand this more closely if we consider the mental processes of young children, and the effects of, for example, abuse on a child's emotional development. Mary Main, one of the leading researchers into Attachment Theory, noticed how children younger than about three years of age are unable to *reflect* on their own thoughts or their own feelings (Main, 1991). In other words, they cannot be objective about their experience. They cannot stand outside themselves and look in at themselves to consider their own actions or feelings. Instead, they experience the world around them in a very natural, unreflective, and concrete fashion (Main, 1991).

Such young children are not able to see things "in the round" or to see things from different points of view. Things are understood very concretely, directly as they are experienced. For instance, a 2½-year-old imagines in a very real way that the bath water running out of the plughole is likely to suck them down too. This sense of the real being totally real, concrete, and one-dimensional is equally true of the way they conceive relationships, so that relationships are understood in one way, rather than in their multiplicity as adults conceive them. For instance, a granny cannot be granny and mummy's mother at the same time; for a young child, she will be either one or the other.

Because young children are so concrete in their thinking, their emotional development is always more smooth if they experience *emotionally consistent* relationships with their parents. Consistency allows children to make intellectual sense of things, and also explains why the emotional and intellectual development of children who suffer abuse is so often disturbed. Children who experience inconsistent or abusive parenting cannot really make sense of relationships where love and violence are mixed up together. Similar confusion occurs for refugee children who experience those figures of authority in their society who have abused and terrorized themselves and their parents.

The inability to "make sense" of troubled attachments is not limited to the experiences of children. Adult refugees who experience extreme violence often talk about the sensation of being "lost" in the moment of violence and being unable to make sense of what happened to them. Frequently this is because what has happened is so strange, unusual, crazy, terrifying, or sudden that it completely overwhelms their ability to comprehend the devastation they experienced in a meaningful way. Just like a young child who always experiences the world in a concrete way, the adult who has suffered political violence or torture loses the ability to appreciate the precise experience of violence or torture "in the round". They are felt in a very concrete way because the mind literally shuts down in order to survive. In so doing, the survivor loses the ability to reflect upon those moments of massive violence.

What also occurs for survivors is the sense that they are completely alone with the experience. This is absolutely devastating, as they suffer a unique and terrifying sense of abandonment in which they feel that nobody, not even the most understanding and loving parent, can really understand and appreciate what has happened to them. As time goes by this sense of loneliness may deepen and feel more strange and terrible. They may find that their sense of basic emotional trust is so upset that they are unable to make new relationships. Moreover, they may find that old and trusted relationships feel strange, difficult, and empty.

Instead of trust, warmth, and connection, survivors feel overwhelmed by horrifying and undigested bits of memory that continually come back in the form of nightmares and terrifying day-dreams that constantly remind them of the horror they have survived. Survivors who suffer these effects often think that they are going mad. In fact, these dreams and flashbacks are survivors' unconscious attempts to "play back" the experiences in an effort to mentally "digest" them. Very often though, violent and near-death experiences are so far beyond their thinking capacity or emotional grasp that they are unable to make real sense of them. At the same time, survivors avoid recalling what has happened because it is too horrible to think about and because it challenges their fundamental trust in the world.

This disturbance of a basic sense of trust explains how once friendly and trusting people may become withdrawn and socially anxious after experiences of extreme violence. In effect, the adult's "secure base" has been destroyed. The secure base is a notion which John Bowlby recognized as fundamental to a child's development and the adult's later ability to provide love and parental care. In Bowlby's view, a baby instinctively signals its need for physical closeness, which the mother provides through her basic care-giving. When a mother (or other primary care-giver) responds appro-priately to the baby's expression of needs, the baby develops a sense that the mother is a "secure base". The child then internalizes a sense of a safe self as it develops. In other words, with good attachments, children take inside themselves a sense of innate security. From this, they can develop a model of a safe, secure, and loving "world" in which they can operate and get their needs met.

The destruction of the "secure base" and the problems of parenting

Overwhelming violence can destroy a survivor's inner belief and experience of their parent's love and attachment, which they experienced as a child. What seems to happen is that the survivor's internal parent, the mother and father we carry around inside us, is devastated because the experience of violence feels so emotionally lonely; because at the time of violence they feel so utterly abandoned, unhappy, worthless, expendable, devastated, parent-less, and alone (Woodcock, 2000). In fact, torture makes people feel the opposite of how it is to be loved unconditionally by a parent.

Consequently, because survivors have lost their own "inner

parent", they lose the ability to feel empathy and to attune to their own children. Instead they are likely to feel vacant, distracted, easily irritated, explosively angry, and disturbed. Consequently, their parenting of their own children may be harmed. Instead of involvement and warmth they may feel preoccupied and distracted.

All children, however, have an innately healthy drive toward development. They naturally seek emotional and physical comfort from their parents and have an expectation that their needs will be met. This means that parents who have lost their own inner parent will be challenged by the child's natural and healthy demands to respond to their physical and emotional needs. If, then, parents who have endured torture and political violence are unable to meet their child's emotional needs because of the emotional devastation they themselves have endured, their children may complain of a father or mother who looks and smells the same as their original parent but is just a shadow of their former self.

What then comes into play is the possibility of attachment failure. This is a subtle process whereby the child is inflicted with the sense that they are no longer held in mind by their parent. This will be evidenced by the sensation that their parents who have always been "there for them", no doubt since before birth, who have been readily attuned to their wide-ranging needs and responsive to their subtle signals of emotional arousal and needs for care, have now become emotionally absent. The child learns to parent himself and to deal with the subtle cycles of emotional arousal and response without the attentive parental intervention they enjoyed before. For their part, parents feel the despair of not being able to connect. How this affects children will depend on their emotional maturity and many other factors, particularly the availability of adult support from elsewhere. But if young children are overlooked it may result in them becoming pseudo-adults, that is, becoming emotionally independent and self-maintaining before they are ready. This can result in a child who loses the emotional availability, flexibility of thought, and playfulness that an unafflicted childhood can bestow.

Therapy—creativity and the healing process

Attachment research shows that parents with clear accounts of their childhood attachments are more likely to be able to attune themselves to their children's needs for closeness. By doing that they provide their children with an experience of attachment that makes emotional and intellectual sense. The process whereby a parent has learned almost instinctively what their child needs, is called attunement. Good attunement between a parent and child creates a space between them where play and intimate language develop. This space between child and parent is the actual heart of the creativity. It is the emotional and intellectual space in which thoughts and feelings are first brought into consciousness for the child and where the child learns gradually, as the years pass, to become reflective and able to dwell on their own thoughts and feelings and relationships with others.

Good attunement and safe attachment are also essential to heal psychological injury. By contrast, torture has been described as the "perversion of the healing relationship". Through torture, security is replaced by terror. Parental love and care is replaced by the deliberate infliction of pain. Furthermore, the concrete way that adults experience violence is the absolute opposite of the playful heart of creativity experienced between well-attuned parents and children.

Violence that is overwhelming cannot be easily symbolized. It is hard to talk about or imagine. It is often too horrible to bring into mind, but for many of those who have suffered torture it keeps coming back as flashbacks and nightmares because it has not been "digested". This throws into focus the central task of recovery for survivors of torture, which is to have a "secure base" where it is safe enough to think about the violent events they have suffered. If they can bear to do this from many different angles the violence can begin to feel less overwhelming and it might then be possible to assimilate or digest the experience. This is a very creative process. It makes sense of why within a therapeutic relationship that is secure enough to explore, and even play with, the horror a person has been through can be profoundly healing. It also explains how such things as art, theatre, and religious ritual, through promoting different ways of seeing and thinking that allow more rounded and less concrete versions of reality to emerge, are also likely to promote healing.

Therapy with devastated parents and children

It is when the parent is unable to take up the child's challenge for attachment that therapy can be especially helpful. When this happens, a good therapist will offer the parent a safe, secure relationship in which they can rebuild their basic trust. Together, they will carefully explore the language and the feelings to describe the loneliness, fear, abandonment, and anger of the violence. They will search for symbols and playfulness between them that will help the parent experience the therapist as a secure and containing parental figure. Through this process, the parent may take back inside themselves a healed version of their shattered attachments. The therapist may also work at the same time with the relationship between the parent and the child, encouraging them to re-explore their playfulness and attachment to each other. This helps the parent because they are engaged in the therapy at two levels simultaneously, as "children" themselves, whose therapist is a sort of surrogate parent, and as a parent, being encouraged to respond to their child.

Children are also tortured and caught up in political violence. They often see their parents violated and humiliated. As a consequence they suffer from all the effects of torture described in this chapter. They may find it difficult to trust, they may be withdrawn and anxious and easily upset. Very often children reveal what has happened to them in the ways they behave and through play and drawing. For instance, refugee children may draw pictures at school of war that are so "true to life" that they horrify their teachers, or they may play in ways that seem odd, like the six-year-old refugee girl who used to curl into a ball and hide under the desk. It was only when her teachers understood how often she had to protect herself from bombs that they understood what her play meant.

As we have argued, children need to enjoy secure relationships, to be understood, and to live in a world that makes sense, in order to develop good attachments. Parents, teachers, and child mental health workers can help this happen if they are attuned to the child's needs, and feel emotionally secure enough themselves to understand the muddles and difficult feelings that a child who has suffered torture and violence will have (Richman, 1998). This was the case with a young girl who had seen many terrifying things as she and her family fled the war in Kosova, including the brutal beating of her father. She then got parted from her family in the chaos and when they were reunited in Britain it was very hard for her and her mother to recover the trusting and close relationship they previously enjoyed. Work with a therapist enabled her to represent what she *felt* had happened. This wasn't only a factual story, it was an emotional story that included her sense of betrayal and abandonment by her parents, and the humiliation of her father. Within the safety of her relationship with the therapist she was able to work through the overwhelming feelings and fantasises of separation, loss, and rejection she suffered. In the process, her mother was also enabled to understand and respond to her child's terrifying experience with love and careful attention, while comprehending her own experience of guilt.

Conclusion: the need to be understood

The psychoanalyst Donald Winnicott believed that children have a basic desire to be understood. He also believed that the child and its mother are a unity and that the child collaborates with the mother in gaining a sense of self and identity. The role of the parent is to enable this through "appreciative understanding" and by relating to the child's external and internal experience (Phillips, 1988).

We can see that for survivors of torture this can be very difficult, because their external world is so devastated and exile may be hostile and friendless. This is why it is so important that refugees are made welcome, and provided with the means to rebuild their lives in a meaningful way. At the same time we know that survivors are not merely passive victims but are resourceful people who will make good use of the opportunities afforded them.

For our part, we also know how hard it is actually to imagine and conceive of torture and political violence, to let it really get to us, in a way that enables us to empathize with the feelings of those so deeply injured. There is a natural impulse to protect ourselves from such experiences. If we do reach out, however, we will understand something fundamental about attachment: that respon-siveness requires resilience, imagination, subtle attunement, and care. The rewards for reaching out are an expansion of our humanity, and an understanding, both deep and rich, that connections forged in adversity can create bonds of enormous value and strength. Recovery from torture and political violence cannot merely be an individual responsibility, but involves all our deepest, collective human values and actions, and a shared understanding of the ways such experiences shape all our lives.

Good attunement and attachment *help* heal psychological injury. Knowing this is important therapeutically when working with survivors of torture and war. In many ways, the "healing relationship" *that can be established in therapy* is similar to the best aspects of a relationship between a parent and child. It provides emotional security and encourages exploration and play.

CHAPTER SEVEN

Human violence is a preventable disease

Felicity de Zulueta

Introduction

Who would believe, amid such violence and destruction, that human beings are actually programmed to be sociable, friendly, and even loving to one another? Whether we are, or not, depends very much on our early attachment experiences, and how we are then treated in the course of our lifetime.

This chapter reflects on how personal suffering may come to be expressed in violent ways. We begin by exploring attachment relations as part of a wider social nexus of family and community attachments, and by understanding the importance of group connections and values in shaping our understanding of our "selves". We then consider how failed attachments may come to be experienced and expressed through domestic violence, violence that is enabled by gender inequalities. Finally, we turn more generally to reflect on the "cultures" of violence in which we live. Societies that culturally condone and legitimate violence, through, say, ideas about "acceptable" uses of punishment, create the conditions of their own destruction.

Violence as attachment gone wrong

Attachment Theory argues that human beings are programmed to seek out the company of significant others, especially in times of danger. But, if we are inherently sociable, how is it that we may come to behave in ways that may injure others? To answer this question, we need to consider attachment behaviour.

We are born with a need to remain close to our parent, who is usually but not necessarily a mother. When we are small, we will do anything to maintain that closeness; we will cry, howl, make a nuisance of ourselves if need be—we will even be bad to get her attention! And why do we do this? Because she means safety. If we are scared we want to feel safe, and life is full of scary people and things. So nature programmed us—like other mammals—to run to mum or get her to run to us when we are frightened or in need of help. In this way our safety is assured.

From the moment they are born (and even before), babies enter into complex relationships with their mothers (or care-givers). As infants our brains become attuned to the music of our mother's voice and the rhythm of her movements, the touch of her hands, the feel of her body, and the looks in her eyes. Her laughter and her pain, her anger and her gentleness, all shape the attachment with our infant selves, and help to make us what we are. There are others around us, too—our father, sisters, brothers, relatives, carers, teachers, our friends and our enemies. They also have had a part to play in how we feel about ourselves and how we see others and ourselves.

It is also the case that humans are born into a social matrix of family and community connections that have themselves developed through the interactions between our species' psychobiology and the natural world surrounding it. In turn, this social matrix operates within a rich cultural system of rituals, language, music, and beliefs that punctuate every moment of our existence. As human beings we have our languages, our rules, our festivities, and beliefs about ourselves as a group and about the world about us. We imbibe this world of sounds, symbols, and attitudes like a sponge; without even realizing it, we share tastes, laughs, fun, likes, and dislikes with other boys or girls, men or women who live within our social group.

And while we become members of our social group by sharing

its values and beliefs, we also acquire a group social identity. Most of us find that we tend to like and dislike the same people as the rest of our group, and develop a perception of "alien others"—those, for example, whose food, clothing, appearance, speech, and colour may seem to differ from ours. "Mum seems to keep clear of them and dad blames them for being jobless and for many of our problems. In the intimacy of family and social group, therefore, I learn to think there are those whose ways of being are threatening to me, my attachments and my sense of self". We might come to challenge this false "construction of the other", or—as we shall see—we may come to use it to sustain our own sense of identity in publicly violent ways.

With time we grow up, at first close to our family and then closer to our schoolmates and neighbours. Through these many and varied processes of interaction and communication, we develop an individual "self", our sense of who we are. Mead defines the "self" in the following way.

> An individual reflection of the general systemic pattern of social or group behaviour in which it and the others area all involved—a pattern which enters as a whole into the individual's experience in terms of these organised group attitudes which, through the mechanism of his central nervous system, he takes towards himself, just as he takes the individual attitudes of others. [Mead, 1934]

Therefore, through the intimate attachment bonds of our family life, the attitudes of our social group, and the position of the family within the social matrix of our community, our social self develops. As this occurs, we become "members" of society. However, how we relate to others in society, how we behave towards others, turns very much on our early attachment experiences.

As we go through life, few of us are spared the pain of loss, rejection, and fear; we can be hurt by those we love and trust, betrayed and bullied by our schoolmates. We may even go through terrifying moments in which we feel helpless and alone. What happens next will depend very much on the attachment instinct we were born with, that longing for mum or dad, that yearning for a hug, for comfort, for reassurance, and understanding. If it comes in good time, we feel better, we feel safer in the world because we know that bad can be made good, that we are not alone, that we are loveable because somebody cares about us. But what if there is no one out there? What if no one wants to hear our cries, no one wants to feel our pain, no one makes us feel safe? What then? How are we to deal with the stresses to which we will be exposed throughout our lives?

Translated into attachment terms, the care-giver–infant relationship is important not only in terms of how we relate to others, but also in terms of how we subsequently endure and react to the stressful experiences of life. Good early attachment experiences can provide us with the capacity for secure attachments and protection against later traumatization (Schore, 1996). Insecure attachment experiences, on the other hand, often come with a potential for violent behaviour, a paradoxically effective insurance policy against subsequent pain and humiliation. The degree to which someone will be violent or self destructive will usually have a lot to do with how much they have been made to suffer in their early attachment experiences (Zulueta, 1993).

For instance, evidence from the "strange situation" experiments (experiments in which infants are separated from their care-givers for short periods of time and their behaviour is observed when alone or back with their parent) suggest that about 25% of infants will show an "avoidant" response to their parent (Ainsworth et al., 1978). (See also Chapter 8.) Having endured parental rejection at times of insecurity, these "avoidant" individuals have learnt to "cut themselves off" from feelings of anger and fear in order to remain in contact with their care-giver. They subsequently show poor self-esteem and frequent unprovoked aggression to both adults and their peers. For example, the cry of another can be a source of such distress to these individuals that they will do anything to stop it, as happened in the UK in 1993 when two small boys, aged 11, killed a two-year-old by beating him into silence with bricks.

And when these avoidant children become adults, their childhood fear and rage can turn against their partners and children or against those "others" that their own social group has defined as unworthy, dangerous, alien, "not like us". Usually, the social group to which people belong will provide the sanctioned outlet for the inner rage and underlying despair of its members by dehumanizing identifiable groups either because of their skin colour, their different culture, their sexual identity, or their religion; society thereby condones their abuse. The bearers of these vilified "cultural" differences can thus provide the target for a social group's inherent insecurities and attachment failures by becoming the recipients of their rage and frustration. Politicians and religious leaders can exploit this tendency in order to whip up social unrest and justify harsh measures of social control. By fostering people's rage and frustration against asylum seekers, Muslims, homosexuals, and "foreigners", politicians and other leaders can deflect people's more justified criticisms and anger against them.

Importantly, then, the template for potential future abuse is laid down in the early attachment experiences of society's children. We can consider this by way of another example. A study by Troy and Sroufe (1987) on nineteen pairs of four-year-olds showed that in all pairs where one of the children had developed an avoidant attachment style, he or she would victimize the other child if the latter was also insecurely attached. What this behaviour shows is that these avoidant children have the potential to be either victims or abusers. They have taken on board, as a behavioural, cognitive and emotional template, the actual relationship they have experienced and can re-enact either the role of victim or of the abuser, depending on their social context. However, it is also very important to note that in the same study, securely attached children did *not* become victims or abusers. This evidence, therefore, suggests that people's experiences of their attachment relationships provide a kind of internal emotional map by which they then unconsciously navigate their future relationships and social behaviour.

Human violence at its worst can arise as a result of the most severe of attachment failures resulting in the behaviour of those 10–15% of infants who display a "disorganized" response to their caregiver in the same "strange situation" experiments (Main & Hesse, 1992). For these children, it is their parents who become the source of their terror and pain. Can the world get any worse than when it is your own mum or dad who terrify you? Everything in you wants to run towards them for comfort and love, but you can't because their eyes are full of hatred or they are in some living nightmare of their own. "Where to go when I cannot run away because there is no one else in the world who cares and I will surely die!" the child cries. (Yes, when we are small we know that we die without our parents to care for us, however badly they do so.)

Such a child is in a state of terror; the natural fight–flight response mediated by the sympathetic system is in full arousal with adrenaline and stress hormones racing through the body. (See also Chapter Two.) But, when faced *with terror without solution*, the child will find herself "freezing". She will go numb and may even experience herself leaving her body to watch from the safety of the ceiling. What her parent does no longer matters. She can feel no pain or fear.

This stage of "dissociation", in which the child disengages from stimuli in the external world, is also natural defence inherited from our primate ancestors. It is a parasympathetic dominant state of withdrawal in order *to survive* and occurs in situations of fear without solution, that is, those helpless–hopeless stressful situations during which animals "freeze" in order to conserve energy and foster survival by feigning death. Such experiences will often need to be "forgotten" or *dissociated*, so that children can continue to turn towards their parents for safety and care, their only guarantee of survival. The price they pay is that these dissociated nightmares from their past become unconscious, "frozen", traumatic memories that can be triggered back into existence to be recreated by those who survived them either as victims or as perpetrators. We can see how this happens in the following case.

A colleague of mine who worked in a prison in England presented the video of a man called Ben. Aged 39, this man was in jail for the murder of his "buddy" when out stealing. His therapist asked him to confront his mother in role-play. We then saw how this large hulk of a man was reduced to a crumpled, terrified child at the prospect of telling his mother to "get lost". When asked how old his mother was, he replied in a tremulous voice "84 years old", and when asked how tall she now was, his reply indicated that she was now much smaller than him. He looked perplexed as he realized both how absurd it was to be frightened of this now frail woman and yet how real his feelings of terror still were, terror of his mother who used to beat him as a small boy. It was, in fact, this same terror that drove him to commit his crime. When taking shelter in a dilapidated barn one wet night, his buddy pointed out that his mother lived up the road and that they could have a much more comfortable night at her place. Ben had been stealing, and he knew—at least the dissociated memory of himself as a child knew—only too well what pain and, above all, what humiliation he would suffer should his mother find out. His fear was such that when his buddy insisted that they go to her place, he killed him (personal communication).

In this manner, the victim of the past can become the bully of the future (Van der Kolk, 1989) if unprotected by subsequent secure attachments or experiences of being understood and valued. Unable to form loving relations, damaged by terror, humiliation, and rage, these individuals usually end up in our hospitals if they are women or in prison if they are men (Fonagy et al., 1995). Their actions betray the invisible wounds of their minds, protections and disguises to survive in a world in which there was no one who cared enough to make them feel they existed in the mind of another.

The shame of feeling a "nobody" is perhaps the most dangerous source of violence (Gilligan, 1996). "Better to be bad than not to be at all" could well be the motto of many potential murderers. And if, in addition, you can become someone in the eyes of your social group by abusing and killing those who are despised and vilified by your society (by colour, gender, age, sexuality, etc.) then what is there to stop you from doing just that? The excitement of having power over another is one way of keeping one's psychological disintegration and even madness at bay. In other words, while most of us are emotionally nourished and held by the attachments we form, some of us hold ourselves together through perverse attachments that enable us to exist without psychic disintegration.

Condoning violence against "the other", "the outsider", is not the only means by which cultural values may shape how we express our experiences of psychic disintegration. Cultural values also play a role in how we establish attachment relationships and condone those very conditions that may eventually lead to attachment failures. For example, in Northern Germany in the 1980s, Grossman and his colleagues (1985) found that one half of the infants they studied were classified as insecure–avoidant (as compared to about one quarter of American infants). This difference was attributed to the cultural values of the mothers in this part of Germany; the mothers had been taught to believe that as soon as their children became mobile, they should be weaned from close bodily contact. The educational ideal in this region was to produce "independent" infants who did not make demands on their parents but who unquestioningly obeyed commands. Such attitudes were similar to those observed by an earlier researcher around the time of the

Second World War, when Hitler was in power. (See, for example, Miller, 2001.) Such individuals would be obedient but would also yearn for revenge, having experienced utter helplessness in relation to their humiliating parent.

Not all individuals whose attachments have been damaged go on to recreate the nightmarish world they have known. Some escape because they may have had one care-giver who made them feel secure. Others may have been fortunate enough to meet a teacher or a relative whose concern and interest opened their minds to realizing that he or she was being thought about and valued. This experience—of being "held" and valued in the mind of another—is crucial in enabling individuals to think about their experience, to make sense of their abuser's behaviour, and to get into the mind of the other (Fonagy & Target, 1997). This ability protects them from repeating the attachment patterns of their past.

So, what can we conclude at this stage of discussion? What can we establish so far about those who commit violent offences? Research in the field of attachment shows strong links between damage to the attachment system and human violence. While around 60% of our population is brought up capable of forming secure loving relationships, another 25% has the potential to bully and hurt if given permission or encouraged to do so. Moreover, nearly 15% of the population is so damaged by trauma and abuse that they may end up as hospital patients or prisoners. Among other things, many of these individuals show changes in how their brain functions early in life (Siegel, 2001) and, if they suffer from dissociative flashbacks of their past traumatic experiences, they show further changes in brain activity (Rauch et al., 1996). This means that damage to the attachment system may affect the way the brain functions, particularly if it happens in the first two to three years of life.

With these scientific findings and others available to those who claim they want to address the current epidemic levels of violence in modern societies, what in fact is happening?

Patterns of violence: they begin at home

Violence can be defined as the act carried out with the intention of physically or psychologically injuring another person. For example, emotional or sexual abuse may not involve physical injury but results in severe long-term consequences for the victims, the reason being that an individual can be both physically injured and injured in terms of their sense of who they are, their self-esteem.

There is little doubt that violence is becoming an increasingly serious problem in certain parts of the world. According to figures given by the Scottish Executive, in the USA, the homicide rate in 1997 was 67.9 per million population and between 1979 and 1991, almost 50,000 children were killed by guns, a figure equivalent to the number of soldiers killed in the Vietnam war. Homicide is the second leading cause of injury and death among children and adolescents and, according to the US Centre for Disease Control, homicide is the principal cause of death in black males aged 15–24. In England and Wales it was 14.2 per million population in 1997. By 1998, the Home Office reported that the rate for violent crime had increased in England and Wales by 40%, almost doubling that found in the USA. Whereas rape and murder rates are still higher in the USA, at levels of 61 per million in the year 2000, the gap is narrowing between the USA and the UK.

While horrifying stories of murder and torture make the headlines, one of the main causes of these tragedies is not spoken about: this is the secret violence of family life, a form of violence our society is only just beginning to recognize. Domestic violence was defined by the 1993 Home Affairs Select Committee Report on Domestic Violence as:

> any form of physical, sexual or emotional abuse which takes place within the context of a close relationship. In most cases, the relationship will be between partners (married, cohabiting, or otherwise) or ex-partners.

Furthermore,

> ... domestic violence can take a number of forms such as physical assault, sexual abuse and rape, threats and intimidation which are criminal offences. In its most extreme form it may lead to homicide. Physical violence may be accompanied by other forms of intimidation such as degradation, mental and verbal abuse, humiliation and deprivation (which can involve keeping women without money and in isolation) and may also include systematic criticism and belittling. The abuse is repeated, often over many years, and may escalate and intensify. The long-term effects of domestic violence can include feelings of guilt, shame, depression and stress.

The UK government recognizes that the prevalence of domestic violence is under-stated, often because the victims do not report these incidents. We also know that women and children are more likely to be abused and even killed by members of their own family than by a stranger. As far as we know, one in five women in Britain experience violence at some time in their relationship, but domestic violence usually takes place in secrecy: one in four women in the UK tell no one and even fewer tell the police. In the UK, two women are murdered every week by their husbands or lovers (Lees, 1997), that is 47% out of 224 homicide victims. Eight per cent of men are killed by their partners out of 426 homicides (Home Office figures for 1997). These figures represent only the tip of the iceberg, and the most extreme forms of abuse carried out on 50% of the adult population.

In one English survey, carried out in Tony Blair's London constituency, one in three women said that they had been punched, slapped, kicked, head-butted, suffered attempted strangulation, or had been struck by a weapon, many of these attacks resulting in injury. Nearly two out of three males interviewed said that they would use violence on their partners in a "conflict" situation which could be as minor as not having dinner ready on time (McCarney, 1996).

Since men are known to commit most violent offences, this has led some to assume that male hormones are the cause of violence. Many studies have in fact shown that although men tend to be more violent, their behaviour is due more to social reasons than biological ones. One study looking at criminal homicide rates in black and white men in Philadelphia showed that men in each category committed significantly more homicides than women of the same group. However, black women committed three times more homicides than white men. This led the author to conclude that the social determinants of violence were more powerful than the biological determinants. Black people were probably exposed to far more traumatogenic experiences than were whites as a group (Wolfgang, 1958).

These men and women involved in violence were themselves once children who were likely to have experienced attachment hell in the privacy of the family home. For those who witnessed their parents' conflicts, their plight would have been appalling, since it is the most traumatic experience a child can endure, that of facing the potential loss of both parents. Furthermore, such children may also have confronted their own annihilation. In the UK today, 2–4 children die every week as a result of neglect or outright abuse (Meadow, 1989) compared to one child a year in Sweden. Infants who are less than one year old are more likely to be killed than at any other time in their life. In the three years up to 2000, 427 cases of children below the age of ten who were killed by their carers were dealt with by the police in England and Wales but only 27% of these cases ended with a conviction, compared to 90% conviction rate when a child was killed by a stranger. The reason for this is that unless there is evidence showing which of two carers harmed the child, then neither can be convicted of or murder or manslaughter (Dyer, 2002). The National Society for the Prevention of Cruelty to Children published a report in 1996 stating that one million children were seriously harmed every year. And, if we look at child sexual abuse throughout Europe, we find that one in three girls and one in ten boys have been abused through physical contact, usually by males known to the family (Halperin et al., 1996). An American study showed a clear link between marital abuse and child abuse (Finkelhor, 1983).

Bearing in mind what we have learnt from research on attachment behaviour, we can state that the essential ingredient in domestic violence is terror, an emotion we do not want to associate with family life. Victims of family violence live in fear of being hurt and even killed, of being humiliated or totally ignored. They learn to cope with this by cutting themselves off from these painful memories and feelings. But their terror remains, as we saw with Ben in relation to his mother. Like the war veteran who, on hearing a car backfire in the street, is taken physically and mentally back to the battle front, victims of childhood trauma suffer from the same symptoms of traumatization and damage to their attachment system, albeit modified by the process of childhood development. Though apparently adult in most of their activities, these individuals have often remained frozen in the terrifying relationship of their childhood. Like the adult "disorganized infants", when they re-experience a trigger that takes them back to their past childhood nightmares, these individuals flip into their childhood state of total helplessness and terror. Even their thinking can become that of the child who believes survival is not possible without the presence of the parents.

Many a battered woman is reliving just such a terrifying relationship: she often cannot escape from her abuser because the traumatized child within her fears death from abandonment more than she fears the beatings of her partner/parent.

Bowlby (1984) viewed violence in the family as a disorder of attachment. The insecurely attached adults, be they "avoidant" or "disorganized", will naturally attempt to recreate within the matrix of the family the kinds of relationships that boost their sense of self-esteem and security—be it through exerting power over the others or by desperately attempting to feel loved. If such behaviours are socially condoned, then the scene is set for familial conflict and the generation of violence down the generations.

Is human violence a treatable epidemic?

It is clear that childhood experiences of violence in the family produce future patterns of violent behaviour, domestically and in the wider social setting. Furthermore, dominant social values, for example, in popular understandings of how we should raise our children, may actually contribute to the likelihood of attachment failures. So, what, then, can we understand about the social context of the family and the role of our culture and our legal and economic systems in propagating or reducing violence? It could be said that current policies and laws continue to prop up a culture of abuse and conflict within the family. And, our social norms and expectations do little to reduce levels of family violence.

Physical violence against wives was seen as necessary for the "well-being" of women until well into the twentieth century. In 1821, a judge called Mr Justice Brook declared that "If a man beat an outlaw, a traitor, a pagan, a villain or his wife, it is dispunishable" (i.e., it is no offence in law). Such a statement was based on the premise that men should rule over those seen as less human which, to paraphrase the judge, included criminals, delinquents, non Christians, and women. The stage was thereby set for the "dehumanization" of the "other" and this, as will become clearer later on, has been an essential requirement for the propagation of violence in society.

As long as those who govern want to retain their power over others, they need to convince those they govern that some people are less human and inferior to themselves. This legitimizes the use and abuse of certain members of society, starting with women. As long as gender inequality is intrinsic to the society, so is dehumanization of the "other". These inequalities, however, like all other inequalities, are injurious to all parties concerned.

For example, even though men still do have the upper hand as a result of relatively better socio-economic conditions, men and women suffer in the process. This is because, in order to be a male, the man must sacrifice his emotional identification with his first love, his mother. To help him achieve this, feminine qualities must be culturally devalued and women must be seen as potentially bad or worthless. In other words, women must be dehumanized, too. This can result in men being less able to empathize with women and turning to sex in order to boost their masculinity (Stoller, 1975). In male-dominated societies, women are pressured to play the part required of them in order to preserve the male's sense of masculinity. As a result, they deny their own needs and are more likely to turn their anger against themselves and their children. Thus, women tend to be the victims, at least in relation to men, and may then themselves become offenders against their own children (Herman, 1992).

One study in the USA showed that 25–30% of men in college said that they would attempt rape if they could get away with it (Malamuth, 1981). One of the most obvious manifestations of the importance of dehumanizing women is the pornography industry. In 1984, 750 million dollars worth was sold to 52 million men (Russell, 1993). With the sanctioning of the male–female inequality through this industry, the template is laid down for the dehumanization of other "lesser" human beings, such as children.

Despite increasing social and political awareness of the terrible plight of abused children in the USA and the UK, these two societies advocate the use of physical punishment to bring up children. As a result, about 84–97% of parents in these two countries use corporal punishment on their children. In a survey of 2,143 families, Gelles (1978) found that violence well beyond ordinary physical punishment was widespread and was said to be carried out in the best interests of the victim. The results of the survey are disturbing: 46.4% of children between the ages of three and seventeen had been pushed, grabbed, or shoved, 71% had been slapped or spanked and about 7.7%, i.e., 3–4 million, had been kicked, bitten, or punched by their parent sometime in their lives. These figures are seen as an underestimate of what takes place, since these accounts were given by the parents themselves. At the extreme end of the spectrum, between 99,000 and 1.8 million children had their parents use a gun or knife on them.

Straus (1991) points out that physical punishment is a universal phenomenon in the USA, since all Americans are involved, either as victims or as perpetrators. This is because punishment is a sanctioned form of violence essential to the "maintenance of law and order". As Straus notes, physical punishment is used by ...

> authority figures who tend to be loved or respected and since it almost always used for a morally correct end and when other methods fail, physical punishment teaches that violence can and should be used in similar circumstances. [Straus, 1991]

The national and international implications of such a strongly enforced belief system is evident for all to see in our current political context.

The evidence is also very important in explaining why some individuals commit violence so easily when given moral permission to do so by those in authority. In the UK, the government refuses to change the law that allows parents to subject children to "reasonable chastisement". This is interesting in light of the evidence that in Sweden, where smacking was abolished in 1979, hardly anyone now advocates a return to physical punishment, whereas before the new law, only 35% believed that children could be raised without beating.

There are intimate connections between culturally condoned violence and violent behaviour by individuals. Our sense of who we are and how we behave towards others starts in the intimacy of family, in the attachment bonds we develop and subsequently transmit down the generations. But these templates of social interaction, these roles we take on as children and later as adults, are also parts of a bigger system, dictated by the history and socioeconomic context of our social group and its accompanying political system. Our own attachment failures play into the roles we are given as women, men, and children within our particular ethnic group. The external world impinges on the individual through the attachment patterns of his or her family that reinforce some behaviours and reduce others. One such cultural norm is that of corporal punishment sold to us as a means to reduce violence. Unfortunately, corporal punishment does nothing to reduce violence. On the contrary, it seems to increase it, and the manner in which it does this gives us a good illustration of how individual violence is but the manifestation of a larger picture and the socio-economic context in which we live.

For example, strong links have been found to exist between levels of legitimate violence and violence against women. Baron and Straus (1988) showed this in a study of an American state where:

(1) Violence was prevalent in the media.
(2) Violence was used by the government through the carrying out of the death penalty and allowing corporal punishment in schools.
(3) There was a high participation in legal violent activities, such as shooting.
(4) Women were eight times more likely to be raped than in a state with lower levels of legitimate violence.

This study is very important because it shows a direct link between "legitimate" violence and antisocial violence.

Another study on attitudes towards war, killing, and punishment of children was carried out among young people aged between thirteen and eighteen years in Estonia, Finland, Romania, the Russian Federation, and the USA. The results showed that American students were more likely than their European counterparts to agree with the following statements: "War is necessary" (20% vs. 9%); "a person has a right to kill to defend property" (54% vs. 10%); "physical punishment is necessary for children" (27% vs. 10%). For McAlister and his colleagues (2001) these results confirm the gap between the US and the European groups in "moral disengagement" attitudes that could lead to deadly violence. Moral disengagement is what we call legitimized violence, that is, the perpetration of violence that is made acceptable by invoking "rights" and "necessities" to provide excuses for the infliction of suffering upon others.

As a direct result of a violent upbringing that ignores our basic needs for love and care, we create in society a reservoir of people who are capable, in the right circumstances, of carrying out violent acts against others.

Milgram's famous study on Obedience and Authority (1974) illustrates this clearly. In his study more than 50% of ordinary men were capable of inflicting severe and even life-threatening electric shocks on another individual when told to do so by a scientist in a position of authority. They did this in order to make sure that the student in the electric chair learnt his lessons! He concludes his study with the following words:

> The kind of character produced in American democratic society cannot be counted on to insulate its citizens from brutality and inhumane treatment at the direction of a malevolent authority. A substantial proportion of people do what they are told to do, irrespective of the content of the act and without limitations of conscience so long as they perceive that the command comes from a legitimate authority. [Milgram, 1974, p. 189]

Zimbardo's experiment with university students produced similar results in a simulated prison environment (Sabini & Silver, 1982). He simulated the prison environment with highly selected students arbitrarily assigned either to prisoner or to warden roles. This study was focused on what people can do when they are given legitimate power over another. In fact the reactions of both groups were so extreme that the experiment had to be stopped after six days when it was meant to last two weeks. The fact that the experiment got so out of hand was indicative of the violence that can be unleashed when the setting encourages people to express their destructive feelings. Whereas some "guards" obeyed prison rules and others went out of their way to help their "prisoners", a third of them were extremely hostile, inventing new forms of degradation and humiliation and appearing to enjoy their new-found power.

What these studies show is that, in conditions where abuse is made legitimate, certain people who have been maltreated in childhood can find themselves re-enacting their abusive experience either as victims or as abusers, depending on the power they have and the context they find themselves in. The human potential for destructiveness would be related to the degree of damage inflicted upon the individual's sense of identity and his or her attachment system. However, another factor is necessary for violence to erupt as it did in the experiments above, and that is the process of dehumanization intrinsic to the experiments. Delgado's (1968) work on aggression in primates indicates that the most essential aspect in the development of violence is related to the personal reception and processing of information through various mechanisms of the brain: an aggressive monkey will not attack a socially more senior monkey.

In Milgram and Zimbardo's experiments, the authority figure sanctions the dehumanization of the "other"; for example, the student who, "in the interest of science" must be taught what is "right" and what is "wrong". For the experimental subjects who experienced corporal punishment in childhood, the authority figure is like the parent who had to be obeyed. But, in this case, the subject can actually please his authoritarian parent by doing to the student what was done to him. Didn't he learn that "might is right"? A similar process described by both Zimbardo and Milgram takes place in the torture chambers of the world, and is often carried out in the name of "law and order", the "fight against terrorism" etc. with the sanction of a doctor.

The importance of corporal punishment in the propagation of violence cannot be underestimated. Being "tough on our children and on crime" in our societies is still what gets politicians into power, despite the fact that there is no evidence that such policies reduce violence at all. So why is it that people still carry on with policies and behaviours that do not work at a time when we appear to be increasingly concerned about the magnitude of violence in our societies?

To understand this paradox it helps to look at the importance of the military in maintaining violence through legitimate means. After the events of 11 September 2001, the government of the USA started a campaign to dehumanize Muslims, both within the US and abroad, for the purpose of war and "defence". President Bush hiked up the USA's defence budget to $43 million per hour or more than $1 billion a day (*Guardian Weekly*, 2002). And, as the media is intimately linked to backing the American military–industrial complex, it has played an important role in convincing people of the need to build up America's military potential. This entire process relies on the dehumanization of the "other", the creation of an "enemy".

With the collapse of the USSR, new enemies had to be found. This resulted in the USA's military industry moving into "the law and order" business on the domestic front, a booming part of the "war against crime". By the mid 1990s, the USA was spending in excess of $200 billion annually on the crime control industry. Hagan (1994) concluded his analysis of the American penal system by outlining the exponential growth in the imprisonment of young minority offenders and the widened range of coercive sanctions that include boot camps, electronic surveillance, house arrest, high security "campuses", and intensive forms of parole and probation.

The horrors of 11 September 2001 provided the military with a new enemy and all that this implied in terms of the dehumanization of the Muslims and preparation for a "war against evil". Once again punishment was seen as the morally correct thing to do, with little interest in whether it would, in fact, have any positive results in terms of reducing terrorism and violence both abroad and at home. The secret agenda was to bolster the current socio-economic system with all that this implies—including fostering further violence, insecurity and dehumanization.

The huge investment in the American military complex has had serious socio-economic repercussions. In the early 1990s, sixty cents of every income tax dollar went to the military while only two cents went to education. As a result, there were 16% cuts in federal funding for education, 49% cuts in federal funding for health care, and 77% cuts in federal funding for housing (Andreas, 1993). This situation persists.

The parallel investment in the prison system has resulted in two million people in prison and another three and a half million people under penal control in the USA on any given day (Miller, 1996). This results in more than 10 million men in custody for part of a year, in any one year (Gilligan, 1996). The current policy is to increase spending on incarceration and this is supported by the Prison Guards Association, which has given millions to politicians for the expansion of the prison industry (Christie, 1995).

While more prisons are being built in the USA and more offenders are being punished by different means, very little is being done to prevent crimes of violence in the home or in society and even less in the prison system. One million prisoners leave prison every year in a worse state than they entered it as a result of having been raped by fellow inmates. Those outside the prison will pay the price of their traumatization (Gilligan, 1996).

The human damage inflicted by the penal system in the USA does not stop here. It severely penalizes drug offenders: the "war on drugs" results in 60% of prisoners in the USA being locked up for drug offences, whether they have committed a violent crime or not, and most of these inmates are African-Americans. This is despite the fact that 76% of drug users are white, 14% Black and 8% Hispanic. In New York State, 92% of drug-possession offenders were Black and Hispanic (Kaminer, 1995). A similar group bias is present in Canada and the UK, reflecting the levels of racist abuse and inequality suffered by these minority populations. The resulting fragmentation of these families and the abuse experienced by their "criminal males" does little to improve the attachment patterns of their children and the levels of violence in these communities, especially as their experience of racist abuse is compounded by the "structural violence" to which they are subjected.

"Structural violence" represents the unequal distribution of premature death and disability. Thus, those who occupy the bottom ranks of society are more likely to experience early death and disability than are those with more income and wealth. The greater the levels of inequality between the rich and the poor, the more the poor suffer, not only in terms of physical health but also in terms of mental health. These deleterious effects are not linked to levels of poverty but to the degree of inequality. So, for example, young men in poorer groups showed increasing levels of suicide, crime, and drug misuse, and increased levels of antisocial violence (Watt, 1996). It is the size of the disparity in income between the rich and the poor that is the most powerful predictor of homicide rate (Gilligan, 2001).

Structural violence is, in fact, far more deadly than violence caused by armed conflict: in the 1970s, 14–18 million people died every year from poverty while about 100,000 died from armed conflict (Kohler & Alcock, 1976). Every day now 19,000 children die from treatable diseases in the developing world, i.e., thirteen children a minute. This leaves out the effects on the social groupings and their ramifications at the level of family life and the children's attachment relationships.

Conclusions

If our political leaders wanted to increase the levels of violence in our societies they could do no better than to follow the current agenda. It is a template for future social unrest, self-destruction, and violence and it is being carried out in the name of Law and Order and the victory of Good over Evil.

The template for destructive human behaviour begins with the making of insecure attachments of family and is fostered and used by those in authority when they require it—even at the cost of suffering in our families and on our streets. Dehumanization of the "other" is the final trigger for violence to become manifest. It allows people with repressed rage and destructiveness to finally express their feelings on those whom their community or those in authority have deemed to be less human than themselves, be they women, children, Jews, Muslims, Blacks, the elderly, or the poor.

Dehumanization and its counterpart principle of "divide and rule" are also central to the process of social control, and inform current economic policies with the resulting effect of generating and sustaining social and economic inequalities. The resultant poverty can be seen as another form of dehumanization and violence.

There is little doubt that politicians, scientists, social policy makers, defence strategists, etc. invest hugely in the notion that human violence is both morally evil and/or inextricably part of human nature. As long as we can either blame the violent or attribute their behaviour to genetic abnormalities, we can punish them or lock then up. To see violence as the manifestation of a damaged attachment system and economic inequality means putting the needs of children, women, and men at the centre of a public health campaign which would, in effect, imply huge changes to the social and political system we live in. Not many will be prepared to struggle for such changes, especially those who have most to lose—the wealthy and the politicians. But how much more violence can we as a species tolerate before we destroy ourselves and the world we live in? As Einstein said, "We shall require a substantially new way of thinking if mankind is to survive".

CHAPTER EIGHT

Attachment theory and attachment-based therapy

Chris Purnell

June was becoming increasingly desperate to get through the checkout and get home. Her two-year-old son, Adam, sitting in the front of her supermarket trolley, was tired and irritable. He screamed in frustration as he struggled to free himself from the trolley seat, and held out his arms towards his mother demanding to be picked up.

There was little that she felt able to do to pacify him as she struggled to pack her shopping into bags. She turned and smiled apologetically to the woman behind her in the queue in response to the disapproving gaze that was focused upon Adam. A man standing behind the woman visibly winced, his nerves jangling, as Adam let out another piercing shriek. June thrust payment for her shopping in the direction of the cashier with one hand and reached towards her son with the other in a further attempt to calm him. The cashier smiled sympathetically as she gave June the change for her shopping.

Thankfully, June put the money into her purse and wheeled the trolley out of the shop. Immediately she stopped and picked Adam, still screaming, out of his seat and held him. For a few moments he continued to scream as she spoke gently into his ear and held him to her, then he began to calm as the physical closeness and her words reached him through his protest. His crying reduced to a whimper as he snuggled against her, feeling reassured and comforted by the physical contact.

Within a further few moments Adam had stopped crying altogether, and only the occasional shudder of his body gave any evidence of his previous distress. June felt herself begin to calm as Adam settled. She sat down on a seat outside the shop and continued to simply hold him as he drifted off into sleep, and then gently carried him in one arm, whilst using the other to push the trolley toward her car in preparation for their journey home.

E very reader of the above story about June and Adam will be able to relate to and locate him or herself in it in some way. It is a story about attachment, and this is something that is important to us all. The need for human beings to be attached to someone who can provide them with safety and reassurance when they are frightened, anxious, or tired was first talked about by John Bowlby, the originator of Attachment Theory.

Bowlby and others have contributed much to our understanding of the ways in which we form attachments, and the consequences of attachment experiences for our emotional development. Importantly, we seek safety and security throughout our lives, and the way in which we are able to obtain these conditions shapes our self-understanding and our relationships with others. In this chapter, we will review the variety of attachment patterns that early attachment experiences generate, and consider how an understanding of these patterns helps both client and practitioner in a psychotherapeutic environment.

Early attachment experiences and attachment patterns

June and Adam had what Bowlby would have described as a secure attachment, relationship, because as soon as she was able to do so she responded to the distress caused by Adam's fatigue by taking the time to comfort him. This enabled him to settle and go to sleep. It is the ability of a care-giver to respond in this way that forms the basis of a secure attachment. It would not have been sufficient for Adam if somebody else in that supermarket had tried to comfort him. He needed his mother because of the specific attachment bond that he had with her—she was the one that he depended upon as a care-giver.

June's response to Adam provided him with what Bowlby called a *secure base*. That is a sense of safety and security which would give him the confidence to explore and interact with the world in the knowledge that June was there to give him physical comfort and reassurance when he needed it.

This basic attachment need for a secure base is so strong that a child will always attempt to develop a bond with its care-givers (usually in the first instance its parents) regardless of how its care-givers respond to it. Where a care-giver fails to provide a secure base through responding sensitively to a child's attachment needs, then the child will adapt its behaviour and develop what Bowlby called an *anxious* attachment.

Let us imagine for a moment what might have happened had Adam's mother been one of the other women in the supermarket queue—the one who gazed with disapproval at Adam. It is probable that Adam would have learned from the earliest age that to cry when he was distressed would not gain him the comfort that he was seeking, but would more likely result in an experience of rejection. In order to maintain any contact with this woman as a care-giver, he would have had to learn to keep his distress under control. He would have learned that he could maintain contact with his mother, and avoid rejection, if he covered up his need to be comforted, reassured, and to feel secure.

The attachment relationship that he developed would be known as *avoidant*; in the supermarket scenario he would appear as a well-mannered child who, in spite of being tired, sat quietly in the trolley. Instead of looking towards his mother for comfort, he might distract himself by playing with a package out of the shopping trolley or by simply focusing upon the surrounding activity in the supermarket. His mother might proudly tell people what a well-behaved and undemanding child he was. And this approval of him would encourage him to develop further his insular and self-contained behaviour because this would help him maintain an attachment relationship with his mother.

Another kind of attachment relationship might have developed if Adam's care-giver had been the man in the supermarket queue who visibly winced when Adam screamed. If that had been the case, Adam might have developed another form of anxious attachment that is known as *resistant*. Picture Adam in the queue with this care-giver: the child gets tired and irritable and his father takes a biscuit out of the shopping trolley and gives it to him to pacify him. Adam, however, doesn't want a biscuit. He wants his father. And so, after a couple of nibbles, he throws the biscuit on the floor and continues to protest. His father pats him on the head and tells him to hush. Adam, finding that he now has his father's attention, cries even louder, demanding to be picked up.

In this scenario, the woman in the queue who gave the disapproving look makes a quiet comment to the person behind her about spoilt, ill-disciplined children. In the meantime Adam's father gets increasingly frantic, being intensely aware of the attention that the protest is creating, but feeling completely unable to appease his son. Finally, Adam's father reaches a point where the screams make him feel so desperate that he smacks his son's leg and tells him to stop screaming.

Having paid for the shopping, Adam's father leaves the supermarket and wheels the trolley holding his still screaming son to the car. As he lifts him out of the trolley, Adam throws himself backwards away from his father, who desperately bundles him, struggling and wailing, into his car seat. By the time they reach home Adam has screamed himself into an exhausted sleep.

The resistant attachment pattern portrayed in this scenario illustrates a care-giver that is inconsistent in his response to his child. He has no clear strategy for comforting his child. This results in inconsistency or unpredictability, the child becoming difficult to pacify when upset, because it never knows just how much attention it is likely to get, or how long it will last.

There is a third type of anxious attachment, which might not be so readily identifiable in our supermarket scenario, but which, along with the attachment patterns described, has been clearly identified by developmental psychologists through a process known as the "infant strange situation" (Ainsworth *et al.*, 1978). This develops out of a child's experiences of a care-giver who, in one way or another, frightens it. The source of the fear might be abusive behaviour or it might be simply that the care-giver acts in a frightening way because of, say, psychotic behaviour, or substance abuse, or alcoholism. In some instances the care-giver's frightening behaviour is born out of their own fearfulness in their relationship to the child. Whatever the reason, the child now experiences a dilemma—*how to maintain closeness and contact when the care-giver that it needs to be close to at times of fear or anxiety is also the source of its fear*. The observed behaviour of infants suggests that such a dilemma results in a collapse of any strategy to maintain proximity to a care-giver (Main & Hesse, 1990), and a *disorganized* attachment relationship develops.

These various types of attachment that grow out of our early experiences are not features of just childhood. They matter for the kinds of people we become. This is because attachment experiences with care-givers lead a child to develop mental representations of how to deal with attachment relationships. Bowlby called these "internal working models of attachment" (Bowlby, 1989). Essentially, an internal working model is the child's mental blueprint of how to handle present and future attachment relationships. For example, Adam's internal working model of attachment with June, his mother, was based upon the knowledge that when he cried she would respond by comforting and soothing him. His internal working model developed out of the many and repeated interactions with his mother over time. As Adam develops—and this is true for all children—his experiences of other attachments either reinforce or modify the original working model, and as we move through infancy and childhood into adulthood, our internal working models become increasingly more complex and sophisticated.

Adult attachments and the process of remembering

Much has been learned about adult attachment through the work of Mary Main, who developed the adult attachment interview (AAI). What Main's research tells us is that for adults, attachment experiences remain with us, and persist at the level of mental representations. (By this we mean the way in which attachment experiences have become registered in the mind.) Furthermore, behaviours that relate to internal working models of attachment in children as described by both Bowlby and Ainsworth, become increasingly complex and representational in the progression towards adulthood (Main, 1991).

The AAI is a method of evaluating attachment patterns through scoring the unconscious responses of adults to interview questions about their childhood. What the method demonstrates very clearly is that it is not traumatic or difficult relationships or events in themselves during childhood that dictate anxious attachment patterns in adults, but rather the manner in which those experiences have been internalized as memories and states of mind.

Adults who are judged to be *secure* are those who are able to give a structured and coherent account of their childhood, and who are able to speak about traumatic events in such a way as to demonstrate an ability to reflect upon them and put them into perspective. It is as though the ways in which these adults were responded to when they themselves were children provided emotional protection from the worst of their childhood traumas, and this contributed to their capacity to develop secure attachment relationships.

Adults with *anxious* attachment patterns, on the other hand, are less able to narrate their childhood story in a coherent fashion. Using the AAI classifications, distinctive patterns emerge.

1. *Dismissing*. In this instance, in giving accounts of their childhood, adults minimize the relevance or importance of childhood experience; sometimes they claim to remember very little about the events of their childhood, or recount those events as normal. In some instances, the accounts that are given by *dismissing* adults will be excessively brief, or they might contain idealizations, contradictions, or unsupported statements. In the case of our supermarket scenario, it is very likely that the woman with the disapproving attitude toward Adam would prove to be dismissing if she participated in the AAI.

2. *Pre-occupied*. Here, their accounts become very entangled and grammatically incoherent. Such adults are unable to bring their accounts of childhood events to a coherent and concise conclusion. Sometimes preoccupied adults appear to become angry or fearful when relating their experiences. Again, thinking about the supermarket scene, the man who winced when Adam screamed could quite likely be classed as preoccupied if he were to take part in an AAI.

3. *Unresolved/disorganized*. In this category accounts, particularly of

traumatic events, become subtly incoherent through changes in discourse or lapses in reasoning. It is likely that what the AAI identifies is the *dissociative* mechanisms relating to trauma.

The AAI highlights relevance, consistency, and coherence of an adult's account of childhood events, and also the capacity to reflect (Fonagy *et al.*, 1997) upon the affective internal state that is generated by memories of these experiences. This reflective function is of immense importance in helping to explain why, for example, an adult care-giver might be unable to adequately respond to the attachment needs of a child. It represents a capacity to know what it is that the child is communicating through an ability to reflect upon the internal affective state that the child's signals generate within the care-giver; the capacity to think about what one is thinking. The child's experience of being understood by its care-giver is key to the development of a secure base. Thus, the child that develops an anxious attachment style is likely to have experienced a care-giver who is unable to tolerate the affect that its expressed attachment need generates inside them. The affect is therefore blocked or reacted to, rather than reflected upon and used to understand and respond to the child's own internal state. Picture the response of the preoccupied father of the resistantly attached Alex in the super-market example, and how this man found it difficult to respond appropriately to his child's distress.

Similarly, the dismissing mother's inability to reflect upon avoidant Adam's attachment needs meant that he had to adapt by suppressing any outward sign of distress, and it is easy to imagine how he in turn might learn not to reflect upon his internal need for attachment.

The capacity of a person to think about what they are thinking will have a bearing upon how they are able to engage in the process of psychotherapy. However, even where this reflective capacity is limited, psychotherapy can still be effective provided that the therapist has the ability to attune to the feelings that the person is expressing and in doing so provide them with the experience of a secure base.

Most readers are likely to be able to identify elements of themselves somewhere within the attachment patterns that have been described, and the research provides a rich framework of evidence-based theory that is of immense value in informing us of what can be effective in the clinical practice of psychotherapy.

Attachment-based therapy

The impact of attachment experiences persists from childhood into adult life. However, while the internal working models that are formed as a result of these experiences become more ingrained over time, they are open to revision and change in the light of later experiences. This was something that Bowlby himself claimed, and it is a key principle of an attachment-based approach to psychotherapy.

The attachment classifications provide a helpful frame of reference for helping a psychotherapist to know how best to respond to people in a psychotherapeutic setting, and it is not necessary to go through a formal interview process and classify people in order to make use of the theory. Usually it is possible for an experienced therapist to get a "feel" for an attachment style, partly from the person's use of narrative and also through the way in which they relate to their therapist and how they deal with their relationships generally.

John Bowlby (1988) identified five therapeutic tasks that need to be addressed when he talked about the clinical applications of Attachment Theory. We shall now explore these tasks.

If you were starting attachment-based psychotherapy, then the first thing you would need is a secure base from which you could begin the self exploration that is an integral part of psychotherapy. This involves your therapist not only paying attention to making their consulting room a safe environment, but also being attuned and responsive to your *internal* need for a sense of safety and security. In order to respond to the latter need, it would be necessary for your therapist to have some insight into, or understanding of, your internal working model of attachment.

For example, in a similar way to an AAI account, a person with a dismissing attachment pattern is likely to avoid going into too much detail about their childhood, claiming that it is irrelevant or unimportant, or saying that they do not remember much about it. They may also normalize their accounts of childhood events—i.e. "I can't say that my childhood was particularly happy, but then at the end of the day, what is happiness and how many people can truly say that they were happy?" In a similar way they are likely minimize the importance of the therapy relationship and their need for it to provide them with a secure base. They would be inviting their therapist to collude with the notion that attachments are unimportant by accepting this view and not responding to their underlying attachment need, and this simply reinforces their internal working model which has been built upon the experience of their attachment needs being dismissed or ignored.

The therapist's skill in offering a secure base involves being able to recognize and respect their client's self-contained strategy for dealing with attachment related situations, while also providing the possibility of a different and more secure attachment experience through therapy.

A clinical illustration of this was a dismissing person who was dealing with trauma relating to a serious illness. He was handling this trauma in a very self-contained and insular manner. Working with him in therapy involved sessions where there were prolonged periods of silence, where the therapist began to experience uncomfortable counter-transference[1] feelings of ineffectiveness and helplessness in her apparent inability to form any meaningful contact with him.

The therapist's temptation was to give in to the apparent lack of progress and abandon further attempts to engage the client in therapy. However, what she actually did was to bring some of these feelings into the therapy by talking about how difficult the sessions sometimes felt, and wondering what these difficulties might be about. This enabled the client to consider that the therapist might be capable of understanding and subsequently responding to his internal state of anxiety, which allowed him to open up and talk a little about his own feelings of helplessness in relation to his illness, and his fears around death and dying. What the therapist had managed to do was respond to rather than dismiss the client's need for a secure base and provide him with a sufficient sense of safety and reassurance for him to begin to talk about his fears.

In a similar way a preoccupied person will use their internal working model of attachment as a means of perceiving that attachments are inconsistent or unreliable. In therapy such a client might be anxious about their therapist's reliability or availability and continually test it through expressions of clinging anxiety, sometimes mixed with angry rejection. The therapist's attempts to provide the client with a sense of safety and reassurance is likely to be continually tested with further expressions of anxiety, and when the anxiety becomes too great it turns into criticism and rejection of the therapist.

For the therapist such behaviour can produce counter-transference feelings of exasperation and an impulse to reject the client and, of course, to do so would simply serve to confirm the client's internal working model of attachments as inconsistent or unreliable. Again, the preoccupied person's need is for a consistently containing response which will help him to experience something that more closely resembles a secure base.

People with disorganized attachment patterns can often appear to have many of the features of the other anxious patterns, or they may on the surface appear to be secure in attachment terms. The thing that they are likely to have in common is an experience of childhood trauma that was potentially overwhelming, and usually where significant attachment figures were the source of the trauma. As already described, this presents a child with the dilemma of how to maintain proximity to care-givers who are either frightening or frightened.

Longitudinal studies (Main & Cassidy, 1988) have suggested that infants who display disorganized behaviour in the "strange situation" procedure at one year old tend to develop controlling or compliant strategies for dealing with those that they are attached to by the time that they reach the age of six. This, I would suggest, provides the basic template that many people with unresolved/disorganized attachments will use in a psychotherapy relationship.

Main (1994) refers to research which suggests that the lapses of reasoning and discourse, which are evident in unresolved/disorganized adults through the AAI, are related to dissociation. This is a process of "passive" coping (van der Kolk et al., 1996), where an individual will psychologically disengage from an extreme threat or trauma from which there is no physical means of escape. This can take the form of simply "spacing out" or, in cases of severe trauma, dissociative identity disorder (DID), sometimes also referred to as multiple personality.

The same attachment needs apply for people who have a history of severe trauma. Judith Herman (1992) proposes that people who have experienced prolonged and extreme trauma often suffer from what she describes as complex traumatic stress. She identifies the creation of safety as the first requirement for people who are to be treated for such traumatic disorders. In other words, they need a secure base and, of course, in some instances where there has been severe trauma, this might on occasions involve making available the sanctuary of a specialist psychiatric unit. Unfortunately, the experience of many survivors of such trauma is of periods of hospitalization where misdiagnosis and inappropriate treatment of their condition has left them with a deep mistrust of the mental health system.

In attachment-based psychotherapy, experiencing a secure base also involves having a therapist who is what psychoanalyst and author Alice Miller (1989) described as an enlightened witness. This is someone who will listen to and validate the person's story of their childhood. This is particularly important where there has been abuse and trauma, and where, as Bowlby said, a child's thoughts and feelings have been "disconfirmed" by care-givers who are unable to acknowledge the pain and hurt that their actions may have caused or their unresponsiveness may have exacerbated. As one person put it,

> I found that my therapy was so important because it was the one place where I could talk about how I felt about my past and know that my feelings would be completely understood. If spoke to close friends, for example, and told them how angry I felt with my father and the way in which I had been treated all my life they wouldn't understand why I was still so angry. They would say that I should put it all behind me and make efforts to mend the rift with my father, but I wasn't ready to do that. In fact I didn't, and still don't, see that the onus is upon me to do this. My therapist was the one person that I could speak to who didn't make me feel that I was making a fuss about nothing and who allowed me to express how hurt I felt without being judgmental about it. Therapy was the only space that I had and without it I don't think that I could have managed to break free of my past.

Another important element of attachment based psychotherapy is the facilitation of the process of mourning as the person works through the memories of experiences of loss during their life. Loss is represented not only by actual physical loss of attachment figures but also the loss of the sort of childhood that might have been experienced had a secure attachment relationship been available.

Mourning is what Bowlby saw as nature's cure for loss. This involves a process of grieving whereby a whole range of feelings and emotions such as disbelief, anger, guilt, and sadness are worked through as the loss is talked about and remembered. The whole purpose of mourning is to allow us to let go and move on. It is a natural process, and this is why it is such an important part of psychotherapy. This is an important point to emphasize because very often people who start therapy have never had the opportunity, or have never been given permission, to grieve, and so they have minimized its importance.

Apart from providing the client with a secure base, Bowlby (1988) identified additional tasks to be addressed in therapy, which involve assisting a person to explore the way in which they engage in relationships with significant figures in their current life. Clients should also be encouraged to consider how their current feelings and expectations, perceptions and actions are influenced by events or situations that took place during childhood. These tasks very much involve helping a person to recognize and understand their own internal working models of attachment, and to gain sufficient insight in order to be able to modify them.

A further crucial task is to explore the particular relationship between the therapist and the client. This is a key element within various modalities of psychotherapy, but from an attachment perspective it involves making use of the therapy relationship as a means of providing a person with a modified and more secure attachment experience. It is about enabling them to use the therapy relationship to gain a glimpse of what is possible in terms of altered attachment experiences, which open up the possibility of change in their wider relationships.

A clinical example of this was provided by a person with a preoccupied attachment pattern who was particularly anxious about an approaching three-week break in therapy due to the therapist's holiday plans. The client expressed a great deal of concern and anxiety about how he was going to cope without his weekly psychotherapy sessions, and in the weeks leading up to the break the client used the sessions to talk about his fear of being abandoned by the therapist.

No amount of reassurance by the therapist about his intention to return and not abandon the client could alleviate the fear. All that he could do was simply allow the client to express his anxiety and help him to understand it in terms of his internal working model and past attachment experiences.

As the break in therapy came closer, the client expressed reluctance to leave at the end of sessions and the therapist, understanding the protest that this represented, interpreted in a consistent way the client's expression of anger. The therapist reassured him that his anger in no way threatened their attachment, and reassured him that he would see him as usual upon return from holiday. The therapist's holiday came and went, and therapy resumed.

The client told the therapist that even though the break had been difficult at times, it had been possible for him to alleviate some of his anxiety by reminding himself of the therapist's reassurances that he *would* return. He told the therapist that this was a new experience for him, and that through it he had gained a clearer understanding of what a secure attachment might be like.

For the client to be able to hold the therapist in mind is important, but it is equally important to able to let go in order to explore new situations and to develop and grow. Another person's description of his therapy provided a very clear illustration of how he experienced it as a secure base when he made the following observation:

> I notice how I am able to leave you here in this room between our therapy sessions. In my previous therapy I found myself to be constantly thinking about my therapist at times when I was faced with situations that were difficult or worrying; it felt almost like an obsession in that I felt completely unable to let go of her. Now, even though I still have worries, I don't feel the same need to hang on to you when I am not here.

Given that attachment behaviour is triggered by external and environmental factors and that the response to this is to seek safety and reassurance, there are times when people who could be considered to be securely attached can still find helpful the secure base that attachment-based psychotherapy offers. Such times might be when a person is dealing with a serious illness, either in herself or in a close relationship, or when a close relationship is under threat through some other form of conflict or separation.

Attachment Theory not only provides a means of understanding and working with individuals in therapy, it also offers a framework for helping with difficulties within family and couple relationships.

John Byng-Hall (1991), a leading figure in the world of family therapy, described how in stable adult attachment relationships there is what he referred to as a "complementary system". For example, when there is a conflict of interests in a relationship, it is handled by one person (usually the stronger) giving way to the more vulnerable other's need for proximity or distance in a de-escalating cycle, even though the demands that the more vulnerable partner is making are unwelcome at the time.

Byng-Hall described a process of distance regulation in an unstable relationship between two people (a dyad) where there is what he calls an "approach/avoidance conflict". He referred to such relationships as "too close/too far" systems. These systems represent anxious attachments and the nature of the care giving–care seeking relationships of the individuals involved:

> In the relationship ... each sees the other as being as powerful as, or more powerful than, the self. Each then feels compelled to take very active measures to prevent the other from either approaching too close, or deserting altogether. If this does not seem to work then even greater efforts, on each participant's part, are felt to be needed to prevent the other from forcing an intolerable situation on an unwilling victim. There is then the possibility of a symmetrically escalating conflict, in which each move away or toward is resisted with increasing force. (Byng-Hall, 1991: 209)

What Byng-Hall gives us is a snapshot of the process that takes place in the various dyad relationships that are part of a close family system where anxious attachments exist, particularly relationships between couples, and parents and their children.

It is possible for couples who have anxious internal working models of attachment to experience a relatively stable relationship because their attachment needs are complementary. For example, a preoccupied partner may feel that their dependency needs are being adequately met by a dismissing partner, whose ability to accommodate such needs comes through their own strategy of distancing from any potential personal anxiety. In other words, the dismissing partner finds it easier to focus upon the other person's preoccupied anxieties, because it enables them to avoid their own. Such a relationship can seem to work fine until something happens to disturb this equilibrium, often in the form of illness or loss. This intensifies a cycle of approach and avoidance, and leads to an escalation of conflict as the partners struggle to maintain a too close/too far relationship.

The diagram in Figure 1 demonstrates this process. It also illustrates what is sometimes seen happening to a client's closest attachment relationship as she or he works through issues in therapy, and experiences increased dependency needs through activation of the mourning process. I think that it is sometimes important to point out to people who are planning to engage in therapy that the process they are proposing to embark upon can seriously alter their anxious attachment relationships. If it is

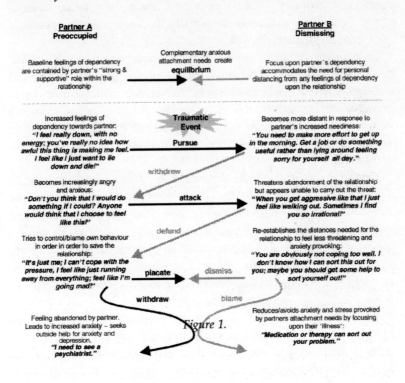

Figure 1.

possible to engage both partners in therapy, then an attachment focus can make it possible to work through the difficulties and alter the relationship to make it more secure.

Johnson's (1996) emotionally focused therapy (EFT) emphasizes the importance of focusing upon attachment needs in couple therapy, and describes how attending to the emotional content of a couple's relationship can be effective in creating a secure connection between them. She points to the difference between primary and secondary emotion in couples' relationships, where the primary emotion represents the reactive response that partners perceive when they seek comfort, reassurance, or a sense of safety in each other.

Such emotional responses might involve anger or rejection or distancing, which can produce similar counter responses in the other partner. The secondary emotion would be the unexpressed, underlying one and often represents the fear, vulnerability, or feeling of helplessness that is experienced when faced with another's attachment needs, or when one's own needs remain unmet. Secondary emotions are usually the very ones that generate a need for secure attachment.

Sometimes couples' relationships deteriorate through critical moments when there has been a failure of one partner to respond adequately to the attachment needs of the other, and although these moments are important, the emphasis in EFT is to move from the content of those moments to an understanding of the *process* that takes place when attachment needs are expressed within a couple's relationship.

Once the process and the secondary emotions are understood, it is possible for a couple use this new understanding to reshape the way in which they relate to one another. Thus, for example, once a partner's dismissing, anxious, or angry behaviour can be understood by both parties to represent an expression of an underlying sense of helplessness or fearfulness, it becomes more possible to find new ways of expressing and responding to the couple's attachment needs.

Johnson suggests that trauma survivors who have a close relationship with a partner can greatly benefit from couple work to improve their secure base. She points out that very often, where a close relationship exists, it is the arena within which repetitions of the trauma are played out, and it is also a primary focus for any potential change in terms of attachment experience:

[A] partner who understands the nature of the terror that takes over his or her spouse is often capable of more empathy than we or the survivor ever imagined possible. Not only that but a spouse or lover is there in the middle of the night when the dragon (the lasting effects of past trauma) comes, whereas the therapist, no matter how expert or empathic, is miles away. The fact that if partners are not part of the solution, they are, almost inevitably, part of the problem, is a cogent argument for couple interventions. [Johnson, 2002]

EFT has proven to be effective therapy where there is a desire by both partners to repair the relationship. Research (Johnson & Lebow, 2000) has indicated that, in most cases, a successful outcome to therapy can be achieved in a relatively small number of EFT sessions, and there is little doubt that the success of this therapy owes at least as much to the evidence base of attachment research that informs it, as it does to the skills of the therapist.

Therapy across the life cycle

There is little doubt that John Bowlby would have been gratified to see the extent to which his original contribution to our knowledge and understanding of the fundamental human need to be attached is continuing to have such an increasingly important influence upon the way in which people can be helped by therapy.

Attachment Theory is something that most people can readily identify with and understand because it has relevance to everybody's life story—from the way which in we form relationships in our early years, through to how we choose and handle our close relationships in adulthood.

When we ourselves become parents, our previous attachment experiences have a great influence upon how we are able to relate to and nurture our children. Even in later years, attachment needs are important as we adjust to the changes and losses that are an integral part of the process of ageing.

The stories that people bring to therapy are often about attachments that have failed or gone wrong. This is why, in the world of psychotherapy, Attachment Theory and research is continuing to gain increasing importance. It is a theory that helps our understanding of a fundamental human need that persists right across the life cycle—literally from cradle to grave.

Note

1. Counter-transference refers to the process by which a therapist exports thoughts or feelings on to the client or into the relationship that exists between them. Sometimes the therapist also imports, or picks up, feelings or sensations that the client might be unconsciously communicating (Southgate, 1990).

CHAPTER NINE

Their daughter, my self:
a personal journey

Anonymous

Editors' note. On a visit to the United States in 2001 to attend a seminar on attachment, Marci Green met up with a remarkable woman. In the course of their few days they shared their views on attachment, they spoke about this book, and the issues that it should cover. Out of that discussion came her extraordinary offer to write this personal account of her experiences of failed attachment and the processes by which she came to establish a secure base within herself with the help of an attachment therapist. We were honoured that she was willing to share this autobiographical narrative and believe it is a fitting chapter with which to bring this book to a close. We are truly grateful for this contribution.

* * *

January 1994

She sits down beside me, collecting my hand. Exposing my wrist to feel my pulse, she says, "Count back from 100, subtracting seven as you go".

I wonder if this is a game, or an entrance exam. Either way, she is waiting. Anxious good will sets me in motion, and so I begin.

"Let's see ... 100, 93, 86, 79, 72, 65" and so on as I find my rhythm. By "34", I've got up some steam when she abruptly instructs me to

"STOP!"

I think she is rude, because I was so close to the finish line. But, I've done what she wants and I feel in control, although somehow I also feel that I have failed. I've failed something because I succeeded. I sensed this the moment she spoke.

"How did you manage that task?"

"Because you asked me to."

"No. I mean, how did you manage, in the state that you're in?"

Well, I AM in a state. Why else am I here ... in this ... this ... What? Haven? Sanatorium? Home from home? Hah! Hell hole! Loony bin? I can't quite fathom that I'm someplace like THIS. My mind is banging hard in my skull, and I want to drill a hole to blow off the pressure. My thoughts don't connect with anything I know and my heart is running a four minute mile. I'm amazed it keeps going.

"Look", I say. "I may be unravelling but my brain still works. My skin doesn't fit but it still contains me. Unless, of course, I'm leaking."

And she thinks about what next to say, as I reclaim my wrist. I sit. Stupidly. Stupefied by the wall. I feel I've let her down in some way. She's struggling for a diagnosis to label my "condition", and here I go making matters worse because I have managed to count despite my confusion. I want her on my side, to tell me what my problem is. I need her to do this so I won't feel lost to myself. I panic at her loss of words. Please don't let me be outside her comprehension. Then she says ...

"You're sick."

I take this in. Then think, Is this the best she can do?

"No," I say, "but I'm terrified. And my mouth is dry. And, I can't remember if I like chocolate."

"Ah, you're sick, then."

"No, but my heart is cracking and my breath is escaping."

"Do you want to die?"

"No. I just don't know how to live."

Now she peels her lip, and removes a layer. She works at this until the bleeding starts. With a lick of what's left she stands up to go. She nods, pops her elbow and then shoots me a smile.

"Your ward's to the left, the recreation area is to the right. Dinner at 5. Pills at 10 and a hot drink whenever you want it. Any questions?"

Questions? Jesus, I'm choking on questions. But I think she can't help. I'm out of her league while she's out the door, and I'm left here struggling for breath. I watch as my hands gather my bags, and my feet walk out the room. My hands, my feet, my breath, my bags, my being. I am in a parallel universe and cannot find the me to whom they all belong.

*   *   *

1953–1975

In the beginning, and then always, there has been family. I live in the East as an infant and child. There's me, an "other" and the voices of strangers. I cry, she comforts. I gurgle, she smiles. I walk, she rejoices. I explore and return, and she is still there. We have meshed with each other so that I can be. Back then I felt safe because she was there.

He's around, too. In my fear of his chaotic presence and delight of his arms. In the smell of cigars and the sting of his belt. "If you cry, I'll hit you again ... and then you'll REALLY have something to cry about." Of course I cry, and get belted again. My fault. Old enough to walk is old enough to be smacked. But I stand on his toes doing foxtrot and waltz. I dance on my own feet and I'm his gorgeous girl.

Mine is a respectable family, with two parents, three kids (with me as the youngest). We are nuclear and intact, and upright in the community. My folks came from an immigrant background and their early life was a struggle. But we are "proper Americans", now, and at a safe distance from Europe. Friday night Synagogue and we weep for those lost. Then we head for the tables of sweet wine and sponge cake. Come Saturday mornings I learn Hebrew, and what it is to be a daughter of the faith. By Saturday afternoon, though, it's hotdogs and baseball. Then it is supper and TV, and the slipstreams of sleep. Tomorrow, and tomorrow, are school, home, and play. These are my routines of childhood, with a family that is all families. Or so I believe. And this is how it is.

For these first several years, there is ordinary peace. And ordinary conflict with my parents and siblings. Sometimes we play games, and I usually lose. OK, I am the youngest and they know the tricks. But I can crawl into small spaces so I win hide and seek. Outdoors in the summer are more places to shelter, and more places to wander, alone with myself. In the winter there is snow, and I am home before dark. I grow, and the spaces get smaller but there is still room to play. Blankets and chairs turn to fantastic tents. Closets have mystery and my parents' stored memories. Closets are good for becoming invisible, but that's where he finds me to share a few secrets. A brother I adore. To tag me, then touch me, and smell his sour salt. I am amazed, and ashamed, and it stings down there. I don't know what to do with this; it is a secret I cannot hold.

I tell my mother. She hears me. She must have done because the touching stops. She's there for me, and I'm safe again. The rhythms of the house are slowly restored, but I now know something I don't like, and it becomes part of me. I take this into the next season of hard, icy winter. But the spring brings sweet flowers, fireflies, and a new Boxer puppy.

I am seven and then eight and some changes are coming. My parents tell us that there is adventure ahead. They want to move West to Nevada to get away from the snow, and to be with my mom's brother whose family lives there. (There are other reasons, too, but I don't think I grasp them.) My uncle is a light in my mother's life and she wants to be near him. She'll also help my dad start a new business in this flourishing town. I guess there will be enough for us all to dream about. My feelings are mixed, but I think I'm mostly glad.

There are many good-byes, and this makes me ache. But the wrench is softened by hugs from a favourite aunt, well wishes and fresh peach ice-cream. I will miss her. My home is now in boxes, and my best friend will become a pen pal. I say "so long" to my street, my house, my bedroom, and bed, and then to the fairies near the pond down the lane. I love the rich greens, and scents of sweet peas. I think, for the first time, that "dapple" is my favourite word.

I have this thought on a soft August day, as we step on to the plane for my very first flight. I like this sensation of safe in the clouds as the sun makes the silver of the airline wings shimmy. And just for being there, I have earned my junior stewardess wings. Maybe I will wear senior ones when I grow up. When I grow up? I think this move is part of that process. Hours in the air and I'm giddy with the future. But then we touch down, and I smell something sharp. Out of the plane on to hot, boiling concrete. My lord. I wasn't prepared for this. I can't breathe, in the heat of this punishing sun. This is heat so hot that it burns my lungs.

I soon come to learn that there is little relief from the sun, as we settle to new lives on a street with no trees. The heat overwhelms and invades, and seeps into private spaces, in a town of sharp corners and burning surfaces. The rhythms of each day are drummed by cicadas and aircoolers. There is too much light, and I feel trapped in a camera's flash. I yearn for the cool dappled greys and sweet creamy greens of the East, tender feet in puddles squishing mud and soft flower petals. But, now we go barefoot on the streets of this desert town, the soles of our feet hardened to broken glass and searing concrete. Where are the seasons and the changes they promise? Here there is no weather, only climate. It is flat, unyielding, and unforgiving, and I am unhappy with this place.

But, there's pleasure in the playground with baseball and boys. And, at least in the winter, the citrus trees blossom. When the fruits ripen, we can pick them for breakfast. They are also great missiles to heave at passing cars. I throw, hit my target and run like hell. I think this is wrong, but it really excites me. Other things do, too, so I flirt with new dangers. I'm getting real breasts and I share them with guys. Of course, I only go so far. But I know other girls who go further.

Things with the boys get me confused. I know what I like, but I'm not supposed to want that. I tell myself that if I don't want that, then they won't want me. But I know that's not the reason for the pleasure I seek. Frankly, I like it because it feels so nice. And that's wrong, I guess. (That must be the case because I can't tell my parents.) I am not the only one who can't work this out as my girlfriends say the same things. But it still makes me worry about the person I am; a girl just about thirteen with Bas Mitzvah around the corner. At such moments, I sense some odd angle with myself and my parents, and am overcome by the need to rebel. Maybe I won't go "all the way", but I like all the other stuff. Not supposed to do any of that, either, because I am told "one thing leads to another". Well, why then do anything? Grown-ups are stupid.

It seems I'm developing what my folks call "an edge". Is this edge hard and sharp, or just a ruche in a surface? "All piss and vinegar, you are," says my dad. Is this who I am, or starting to be? Is this a bad thing or something I should cultivate, especially since there is something about this he seems to like? He is a man who lives life in combat and I am his foot soldier. We stand together, him and me, taking shots of whisky when he comes home from work. He is girding for battle, with ghosts past and present, and he's suing the world because his business is failing. He paces the floor, for hours every night, nursing his grievance and a burgeoning ulcer. He needs me to be on his side, and I struggle to be there.

My mother is scared, and tries to help my dad recover the business, but discovers things about him that are too much to bear. She retreats, when she can, into the comfort of her brother's family. That is, until they move away. Off to Colorado. His departure is hard for her, and although she has her children and a handful of friends, I think we are not enough. I observe as she sits with her friends—well, more like at the edge of friends' circles—chin in her hand and pain in her eyes. She is reaching some limit, with my dad and herself. And she's reaching some limit in her "thereness" for us.

My brother and sister disappear for long hours, as they take flight from the arguments, broken glass, and bereaved hopes. I'm stuck at home, or the school playground—still too young to cruise in friends' cars and hang out at the shopping mall. At least the family can all meet up for supper. But, each meal becomes an endurance test and the first course is anger. From this we retreat, into the rooms of our own uneasy company or the company of friends whom we rarely bring home. No surprise that each of us has an ulcer.

My mom gets a job. It's not just the money. She needs more than what she has at home. I try to help out so I start to make suppers. I fear that she'll leave us so I work hard to do this well, in order to please her and keep her with us. Deep down, I yearn for my mom, but she is out of reach. I smile, she frowns. I dance, she looks away. I'm frozen out. Where is there to go but to seek out my dad, and ride out his anger for the moments he hugs me. Still his gorgeous girl? Only when he's in the mood.

We now avoid home, and I'm old enough to make my own way. I still want my parents but I somehow can't reach them. The harder I try, the more distant my mom is, and the more demanding and erratic my father becomes. I am now turning reckless, and am aware of the risks. I like me and scare me at the same time. They say I've gone wild, so wild I shall be, but I still do my homework and manage "straight As". Let me say, too, that I'm not as boy crazy as my mother insists. (She has this thing about me and sex.) I come home one night with a rip in my new blouse. The truth is that I was just dancing with a friend when his school ring caught on my sleeve and tore it. My mother doesn't believe me. She erupts, beats my face and calls me a whore. She does this because this is her truth. And, in her gaze, I cannot hold on to mine. *I give up my truth for hers. Anything to stay connected.* But, who needs them anyway because I'm almost invincible, and seek out new dangers. I hang out with guys who go looking for trouble. And then I spend an hour in the back of a police car, "What's a nice girl like me doing in a place like this?"

Now my name is on record, and I have dishonored the family. They punish, and worry, and punish again. At least in this way I manage to touch them, and I hope that they'll be there if I suffer enough. But, I'm the daughter gone wrong who just can't put it right. "And how could you do this, in Holocaust memory?" Ah, I'm a monster, with a self that's out of control. This is their truth. And the more they believe it, the less they can hear me. My own truth is silenced and my injury buried. No point in my protest, since each protest is punished. My own truth is too risky so I choke on my tongue. I guess they are right, but how can I live with this?

Slowly they go, as I grow through my adolescence. My brother and sister move on to a different life. This leaves me, and my folks, and a roomy spare bedroom. This is the space now offered to a favourite nephew, just out of the army, so he can come to the local university and save on expenses. I liked this cousin when I was a child, and he has grown to be a handsome man. Six years older than me and he seems so worldly wise. There's darkness in his eyes, though, and a deep brooding manner. The local girls like him, but some bit of him scares me.

It's a month since he's moved in. He has been good company since my sibs moved away. But he now takes an interest in me that doesn't feel right. One evening—a lingering touch on my shoulder and back, a lingering look as I head for my bedroom and sleep. Another evening—knock on my door, just to say, "sleep well". Then a knock on my door for a bit of a chat. Then no knock on the door, just a door slowly opening. I think I am dreaming, then I know I am not. I ask him what he wants, and he tells me he thought he heard me crying in my sleep. On each successive night, his reason for being there changes. It's hard to get a handle on this, 'cause he wants me to believe that he's there because I need him. Nothing to do with him, of course.

My parents are away for the weekend, and I am feeling unsafe. I lock the bathroom door but he picks it open. I'm covered with a towel, but I'm still far too exposed. I don't want him near me, and ask him to leave. He listens to me and walks back out the door. This time. I dress, leave the house, and don't return home till my parents come back.

I don't want him near me. I am sixteen. I would like it with someone ... eventually. But not now, too soon, and I don't want it from him. I have said this to him, and he leaves me alone. But after some weeks, his games start again. In the middle of the night or in the morning once my folks have left for work.

It seems he can't hear me say "NO", though I am perfectly clear. I can't lock him out of the bedroom—no locks are allowed on the bedroom doors. I shake and feel queasy, and find reasons not to come home. But my parents punish me for staying out too much. They ground me, for days, which then become weeks. (For my own good, of course, because I am out of control.) This pins me to the house ... and in his reach. And then I am pinned by hands and his mouth. This is vile. But I am overtaken. First by his body and then ... by my own desire. A sensation so strong that I seem to implode. Oh. What force. So THIS is an orgasm. So swamped by such pleasure. But how do I have this, in this ghastly space? What exquisite collapse ... but I have betrayed me.

I guess that it's true what they said all along—I'm wild and a danger to me. I'm clearly as bad as they made me believe, so I need to be rescued from him and from me. I seek my parents' help and I need them to listen. I search out the moment that will make all this change. One night, after dinner in the living room, I sit on the best couch, and tell them what he is doing. They have asked for the whole story and I tell them what I can admit to. They sit, in some silence. Don't they believe me? They then rise and move off, walking slowly through ether, to knock on his bedroom door.

He answers, and they ask for his truth. But why are they ASKING him anything? Don't they believe me? (Maybe, on reflection, they were seeking a permission to unhear this. He is family, after all.) He lies and denies, and then shuts the door.

They stand in the hallway with their thoughts too big to hold, and stare at each other in disbelief. They are silent, and frozen to the spot on the landing where once I spilled cocoa. I need their certainty that I am worth saving.

Don't hesitate, please. Don't let my moment for rescue slip out of your grasp.

I wait in their quiet and my heart heaves toward my belly. They are taking too long to find a way through this. And that's long enough to send me to hell.

So what if he packed his bags and left that night. (And, who knows what story the rest of the family will be told?) By the time he was out of the front door, I had tasted oblivion. I needed, but couldn't have them, and couldn't make them there for me. Maybe I should have tried harder to make me OK; maybe then they would have acted without hesitation. Now, I have only me. But what kind of me am I that makes them uncertain? What kind of me am I that served up my betrayal.

That's the beginning of the next few years. Somehow I pass through them, unclear of my shape and a stranger with my parents. I am isolated. This is both hard to bear and a comfort. And I worry. Is this it? Is this normal? I don't think I can cope.

I taste metal in my mouth, and my breathing is shallow. There is a vice around my head and I'm seeing through gauze. My head feels clogged, There's no room for movement. They say this is a breakdown. (It will be the first of two.) I'm nineteen. My parents are there for me as well as they can be, but there's now too much in the way. Others say, "Don't be so selfish." "Pull yourself together." I would if I could, if I knew where the strings were. And with this I go on to university, shuffling to classes, with a bottle of Thorazine. I just can't continue, and bring myself to a halt. How can I think of my future? I can't do this. I can't do anything, but breathe through the sound of a life expiring. I see a shrink. The Master-Controller. I hate him, but I guess he will put me right. He will help me see sense once he has told me what is wrong with me. At least he is listening.

I think months have passed, and I can barely move. I am groggy with pills and have fog in my brain. But then I go out, in search of, I don't know. This is some moment of defiance and a declaration of self. And with that, my first "proper" sex. It's not quite on my terms and it doesn't feel nice, but at least it was something that I initiated. But holy shit. I become pregnant. Well, I guess that will show them! But maybe it won't. I think that it only confirms my worthlessness. Oddly, however, I feel in control, and the fog in my brain starts to lift. I get an abortion, and then taste their fear. How curious; this power somehow gives me direction.

I turn back to my books and manage to study. Words are a refuge and I rejoin my course. My vision expands to a country imploding. We are still in Vietnam, and I'm against the war. I feel I am against most things, but I'm not sure why. I start to breathe easy in public spaces, doing battle for others, if not for myself. I now feel much stronger, and then get my degree. I've achieved with distinction, but I think at some cost.

I have also left home, to live with a man, swapping my parents for a black eye. Then, my mom leaves my dad and sometime later, I leave the man. I am a woman seeking exits while friends seek marriage. I leave his house, and leave that town. And one year later, I head back East, hoping to put distance between them and me. I take what I can carry, including myself. I just don't know if this is good thing.

The East 1975–1980s

I loved this small town—a place in New England that brought me back to the seasons. Ah, dappled. I came alone to do graduate work and it was hard. This was my refuge, though, and I felt safe. A place to study and play in puddles. I had little money, but the library was free and warm. When that closed, the late diners would do. This kept me in coffee and good conversation. I met nice people, as lovers and friends, and lived in a succession of meagre studio apartments. I stole what I ate, to save money for heating, but this was all part of the charm. The winters shocked me, but I was salvaged by spring crocuses, daffodils, hyacinth, and lily of the valley.

I wrote to my folks and got letters in return. (My father's were stained with tears and blood.) They wanted and missed me, and needed me home. My family loved best at great distances, and I returned the feelings in equal strength. I wanted and needed, but couldn't go home. Like them, I was connected through distance, and the greater the distance the safer I felt. What was my life like, they wanted to know. I shared what I could and was glad for their interest.

My books were my sanctuary, and my politics sexy. Most of living, though, was whatever it took to get by day to day. I got cash from the odd typing job, and a bit of some teaching for short bursts of time. So, I imagined myself as a literary hero (romantic, not tragic), gripping a pen by the light of the gooseneck lamp.

I got another degree and a responsible job as a teacher at a local college. I seemed to connect with the students, and this made me feel so good. I felt in control, but not wholly at ease. Who was this person my students sought out? Was I that wild child, who now sat marking essays? Was this me more real than the one I had been required to be? I managed enough to navigate my life, and much of the time I felt easy in my skin.

Until I fell in love. He was clever, and a crafter of ideas and words. A man with opinions, by whom I could set my compass. He'll keep me controlled whenever I slip. Connected and connecting, I was stupid with joy. Together, we were a couple, of independent people. My companion. My heart. It had all come together. The man, then the house and the regular income.

Together enough, but the connection was fragile. Some old unease was beginning to bubble. Growing in boldness, a sense of foreboding that leaked in through my skin and into my lungs. There were moments I couldn't catch my breath as old feelings of panic became lodged in my chest. Somehow, my loving became something to dread. Ah, but of course; I love best at long distance, so I was now at risk. He, too, loved at a distance. So, in that we were well matched.

I thought I had grown out of these feelings, this free-floating fear at the centre of me. I thought this was all behind me or at least four thousand miles away. I thought I had charted new routes of emotion, and in a way this was true, but the old feeling maps were tattooed in my body. The contours of childhood ways of relating still shaped me and patterned the space that I occupied with this good man.

And slowly and slowly a crisis accreting, my compass came adrift. We decorated rooms of the house that we shared, but we came to live disconnected. He was, like me, a person of exits, trusting too little in the "thereness" of others. This, though, we declare, is to be embraced so we won't succumb to "bourgeois values"; my interior life embellished by culture. I was suffering despair, but despair was so-oo sexy. It's "good to have angst", because it means I've grown up. We celebrate non-dependence because that makes us adults. But wait. When loving is so essential to life, why does "to be adult" mean to diminish our need for others?

My skin couldn't hold me, so I had to seek help. A nicely dressed man who gazed out the window and rocked back on his chair. There was always food in his study, and his services were free on the college health plan.

"The problem, my dear, is being "too needy". Now that you're an adult, you shouldn't need others. That is dependency, and that makes you weak".

I sit and ponder this.

"Oh, OK. If I make myself need nothing, will I soon feel better?"

"Well that depends on which needs you let go of, and which ones you keep."

"How do I know which is which? Is there a book I can read that will tell me what to do?"

"No. But it's not difficult. We'll just help you let go of your dependency needs."

"And then?"

"Well, we look at your other problem. That is, you don't know how to commit."

"Now I'm confused. If I don't need others, then to what do I commit?"

"You commit as a grown-up. You become self-sufficient and leave the child's needs behind. The past is the past and you must think of the future. The sooner you can do that, the better you'll feel."

"But I am the past, and all that I have to move on in the future is stuck there."

"Uh, your time is up. Let's discuss this next week."

I edited this version of a year's worth of "work".

* * *

The Interior—1980s–1990s

After a year of counselling, I just could not go back. It was like so many others I'd had in the past. I was a good at this game of "naming that pain", but on all such occasions it was just my vocabulary that developed. I could play with the words, leaving feelings untouched. I stopped seeing him because he gave me no hope.

I was a wise-ass, a wiseacre and wise-cracking mess. And that's how I got through my days. I was good at my job, but unhappy with me. Fresh paint on the walls, and a new landscaped garden. A relationship embellished with things we could buy, but a pain going deeper than some new plants could fix. Days at the gym, and my nights running sidewalks. Physically fit while I'm falling apart.

I started yet another degree, a new set of books and a place for retreat. My relationship was breaking and I didn't know how to stop it. I couldn't stay, but was too terrified to go. What, after all, was there "there" to take with me. I brazened it out with some pithy one-liners. I wore these as armour, but they failed to protect me. I longed for some rescue, but experience had almost demolished the belief that living might one day feel better. Maybe one last attempt, a woman therapist recommended by my physician. I hovered with anxiety at the thought that she couldn't help. Could I risk finding out that no help could be had? But I so needed someone that the risk was worth taking.

She worked at a Health Clinic in the next town. In the twenty-minute drive that was taking me there, I struggled for a description of me that would attract her interest, while looking for ways to prevent my exposure. By the time I got there, I was a bit of a mess, and just able to sit in the waiting room outside her study. I counted my fingers, from left and from right, and then looked up to watch as a stranger approached me. Her hand was extended to welcome me here, and her smile was as large as the pain in my heart. That smile, an invitation; I was relieved I could respond. But I checked my defences and held her at bay. We went to her room, and she quietly waited. A respectful audience. I sat down slowly, and offered the only bit I could muster.

"This is my life. I can run the film. It's called, THERE'S SOMETHING WRONG WITH ME."

And the conversation began. The two of us, together.

I asked ...

"Can you fix me?"

"No. But I can work with you."

"Can WE fix me?"

"You don't need to be fixed."

"Of course I need fixing. I am a bad person. I'm too needy, can't commit and am stuck in the past. I'm wild, dangerous, and out of control. There's something wrong with me."

"There's nothing wrong with you. You are very right."

"That can't be true."

"Whose truth is that version of you?"

"I think it is mine, isn't it?"

"Well, that's something we can discover."

"If it isn't my truth, if I am not those things, then how come I feel so awful?"

"I don't know, yet. The details have to come from you. I haven't lived your life, you have."

"What kind of details will those be?"

"Whatever you feel is relevant."

"But relevant to what?"

"To whatever it was that made you believe those things about yourself. That made you believe there is something wrong with you as a person."

"How could I ever believe otherwise?"

"Why don't we try to find out."

"Who are you?"

"A human being. And a witness."

"This may take some time."

"I'll witness for the duration."

"Do you want to see the film? It's edited?"

"No need to edit. Take as much time as you want."
And I did.

*   *   *

Into the 1990s

It took many years. This was no quick fix. Time for telling, and
giving testimony, and time to value the child I had been. Time for
testing both my therapist and me. With my therapist, I began to
know me, in a way I hadn't before. We unpicked the embroidery of
events and perceptions. We worked back through the stitches of my
poor sense of self. Me-in-relation. Me-attached. The child in need,
but the child's needs not met. Never too needy, just perfectly
ordinary. The need for connection, but connection gone sour.
Knowing that my parents were unable to "be there" was a terror too
big and one that I buried. I blamed myself because that was safer ...
and, at least, maybe then I could put it right. How do you live
attached, when attachments have failed? When you'll buy any
version they give you just to stay in their care.

Gradually I came to the heart of my truths, learning the
difference between the stories of ourselves we devise to survive, and
the truths they conceal because to know them feels risky. This was a
painful process, and the closer I got to me, the greater the anguish.
To learn and live with the truth is to know what is false in the
stories, but the stories had been written with my mom and my dad,
and to lose those fictions, so I thought, was to lose my parents. And
for so long I struggled to know whose version of me was real.

In the course of this journey, I took hard decisions. With half of
me sober and the other half numb, I left this man and made a new
home for myself. I also found another job and then finished my
degree. With a new sense of me operating in the world, I produced a
book and established a new community of friends and lovers. But
each choice was a challenge so huge I could hardly see beyond it.
Each movement occurred with my hands and feet bleeding as I
dragged me across the sharp shards of risk. If only I could know
which "me" was directing my life. Was this the OK me, or the one I
shouldn't trust?

"There's something wrong with me," I insist with my therapist. "I'm wild and bad and out of control."

Then we reflect. *I had bought that idea in order to live; this was their version of me and I could hardly reject it.*

"There's nothing wrong with me," I also declare. *That is the truth that I buried to live.*

Locked in combat, me and me. If I'm really OK, and there's nothing wrong with me, you'd think I could let the untruths go. But letting those go felt like losing a self, one that was shaped in relation to others.

This conflict became a crisis, and it overwhelmed me. I was my lies and my truths with equal conviction, and the walls of my house resonated with the pain of my struggles. Can't stay here ... can't stay with me. I need to be safe. Must go somewhere else. I made that choice to enter the hospital, and let that nurse take my wrist as I began to count. She wasn't the only one surprised I could count.

Counting back from 100, subtracting seven as I went. This was some place where past collided with the present. The present was about all I could hold, and the future was impossible to imagine. Just let me breathe, slow my heart, and take the ash from my tongue. Rendered helpless, by me. The word games were gone, and now I was overtaken by all the original yearning and fear, as if now were then.

For several weeks, I could not find the person I thought the past few years had made me. These were weeks when the bare present was nearly absent. The corridors of this building were clogged with the debris of a 1,000 childhoods, and littered with pills and cigarette butts burned down past the filters. What little comfort there was for anyone of us in that place came from others engaged in similar struggles. Shadow-boxing with the past. But, at least for me, was the presence of my therapist. The hospital considered her an outsider, but we bent the rules to our own necessary ends and she came to see me almost every day. She helped me hold my good self in the face of my own ferocious opposition. She let me grip her hand as I crawled my way back to me. This had not been a breakdown, but a breakthrough. And she was there.

The more securely she was there for me, the more secure became my base within myself. The more steadily she was there, the more readily I could find me. I left the hospital and moved back out into the world. "The world", at first, was simply my house, but at some time I reclaimed my life. This powerfully forged attachment with her was essential to this process, but she had no investment in keeping me in therapy. This was a secure attachment, one based on the conviction that we work together to discover the safe self within me. She was there as long I needed her, as long as it took to be there for myself. And as I came to learn I could be there for myself, the more able I was to be there with and for others.

That sense of safety did not come overnight, but emerged in a long process of struggle. At least now, with my therapist, words were a tool, not a defence. The feelings could be trusted to show me my truths. And these came. As a letter, a syllable, a word, a phrase and then, a full sentence. "Maybe I'm really OK." And with that proposition, new things became possible.

This was a journey of extraordinary discovery, and harder than anything else I had done in my life. I am convinced it could not have been done alone. I travelled with an "Enlightened Other" who believes that we become who we are *in relation to others*, and that the quality of our early attachments shapes our capacities to develop a secure base within our selves. Through this experience, I eventually came to honour myself, and the processes by which I developed in relation to my parents.

Importantly, I also came to understand that my parents, too, were as they had become largely in response to their own attachment experiences. They did what they could for me and my sibs, and it was genuinely beyond them to do better than they did. Now, with the part of my heart free to let go of "blame", what could I discover about them that made them the parents they were?

*   *   *

Summer 1926—one small piece of the puzzle?

The newspapers, I've been told, got it wrong. Headline stuff. Couldn't even get right the names of the children. Small time bookie murdered for messing the patch? The motive is rarely the cause, but who cares. What a scoop! What a sensation! Who's got the camera? At least the press waited for the family to be informed.

A warm summer's day, and the telephone rang. My grandpa, dead. My mom and her siblings, ushered upstairs to play. He is never coming back, and they don't know why. No space for questions, Ever. Silence, and terror, and the struggle to make sense. A resounding absence, and the world came undone. What was to be done with this? This was a loss so violent that its name could not be spoken. His life—cut in mid-sentence.

This is all I know, and it isn't much. And most of this I just recently learned. I had known he was murdered; shot in the back and left in a dockyard. He was in a violent business. For most of my life, the murder of grandpa was just "an event". For all of my life, my mom kept her silence. Most of her past was out of my reach, and no constant pleading would change that.

When, though, I understood that my childhood attachments shaped who I became, and that this must then be true for my parents, the murder of grandpa became part of me. His youngest child in a traumatized family became my mom. A woman closed down but desperate for comfort. So, I wondered. Did those men who murdered my grandfather help shape the mother that this daughter became? What did she do with that violent death?

A hunch. A guess. Just a piece of a puzzle. A phone call to my aunt, my mother's sister. Questions that make her uneasy. She needed time to think. She then rang me back, and cautiously said,

"I'm ready to answer your questions."

"Do you mind telling me what you can about grandpa?"

I can feel her touch as she quietly begins.

"A summer's day—August, I think—and the telephone rang"

"What were you told?"

"Only that my father was dead and we should go upstairs and play. Same thing on the day of the funeral."

"But afterwards. When you all talked about it, how did you understand it?"

"We never did. Talk about it, I mean."

"What do you mean, you never talked about it?"

"Never."

"What, never?"

"No ... Never."

"What did you do with the experience?"

"I don't remember. I just can't recall. I didn't even know how he died. Not until much later. There was just silence."

"And then what?"

"I went to school, and then I grew up. And that ... was that."

This was more chilling than I ever imagined it would be. The sudden loss, and each alone with themselves. Then later they came to know that this loss was murder. They got on with their lives, but with what kinds of limits?

"Did the world feel unsafe?"

"For whom?"

"For you, for my mom?"

"I don't know how it felt to me. I must have buried it. I don't remember feeling. But it could have been that for your mother."

"Such things can shape the people we become, yes?"

"Yes, that's very possible. But that's not the whole story."

I know there were other things. In my mom's life, growing up in a family barely able to acknowledge their loss. My mom adored her older brother; he became a kind of father. She lost him, too. Then she had to cope with my dad, and his lifelong tango with failure.

"There will be so much more I can never know, but it will have influenced who she became and how she related to us, yes?"

"That sounds reasonable. Why do you ask?"

"Because maybe if I can understand something about my mom, maybe I can live with who she was with me."

"It may. But, remember, as my sister, she was different from the mother you experienced her to be."

And, of course, my aunt was right, and who was I to say what did or did not make my grandfather's child a particular kind of mother to me. But whatever my guesswork and the fiction it might generate, there is still something about which I am convinced. That my mother's experience of attachment and violent loss will have shaped the kind of parent she became. There was that, and then other things, beyond her control. An economic Depression—how did they live? Then the Holocaust and the loss of the family that had remained in the Ukraine. A marriage gone sour, with three kids to support. Unsafe selves in unsafe worlds. Society, culture, biography, and biology. Imbricated. Enmeshed.

My mother did what she did because it was all that she could do. And that she did with courage. Of course, I still want the buck to stop with her, with them, and, in a way it does because those were the people with whom my own life began. But, in a larger sense, the buck has wider circulation—with friends, community, politicians, and pedagogues.

In relation to mom, then, I also did as best as I could do. Our attachment didn't determine the whole of who I became, but they were the girders, the heart of my foundational structures. The same was true with my dad. He did what he did and found it hard to do otherwise. But his is another story about which I know even less. Except, he lost both his parents as a young boy. I do know with certainty, that he hurt all his life. None of us could put it right, and he never let us forget that.

*   *   *

The future

This is now possible.

REFERENCES

Ainsworth, M., Blehar, M., Waters, E., & Wall, S. (1978). *Patterns of Attachment: Assessed in The Strange Situation and at Home*. Hillsdale, NJ: Erlbaum.

Ainsworth, M. D. S., Blehar, M. C., Waters, E., & Wall, S. (1978). *Patterns of Attachment: A Psychological Study of the Strange Situation*. Hillsdale, NJ: Erlbaum.

Andreas, M. D. S. (1993). *Why the US Can't Kick Militarism*. Philadelphia, PA: New Society Publishers.

Arber, S., & Ginn, J. (1991). *Gender and Later Life*. London: Sage.

Baron, L., & Straus, M. A. (1988). Cultural and economic sources of homicide in the United States. *The Sociological Quarterly, 29*: 371–390.

Baron-Cohen, S., Tager-Flusberg, H., & Cohen, D. J. (Eds.) (2000). *Understanding Other Minds: Perspectives from Developmental Cognitive Neuroscience*. New York: Oxford University Press.

Bowlby, J. (1969). *Attachment and Loss, Volume 1: Attachment*. London: Hogarth Press; New York: Basic Books; Harmondsworth: Penguin Books, 1971; 2nd ed., 1982.

Bowlby, J. (1973). *Attachment and Loss, Volume 2: Separation: Anxiety and Anger*. London: Hogarth Press; New York: Basic Books; Harmondsworth: Penguin Books, 1975.

Bowlby, J. (1979). *The Making and Breaking of Affectionate Bonds*. London: Tavistock Publications.

Bowlby, J. (1980). *Attachment and Loss, Volume 3: Loss: Sadness and Depression*. London: Hogarth Press; New York: Basic Books; Harmondsworth: Penguin Books, 1981.

Bowlby, J. (1981). *Attachment and Loss, Volume 3: Loss: Sadness and Depression*. London: Penguin.

Bowlby, J. (1982). *Attachment and Loss, Volume One: Attachment*. London: Hogarth Press.

Bowlby, J. (1984). Violence in the family as a disorder of attachment and care-giving systems. *The American Journal of Psychoanalysis*, 44(1): 9–27.

Bowlby, J. (1985). *Attachment and Loss, Volume 2: Separation*. London: Penguin Books.

Bowlby, J. (1988). *A Secure Base: Clinical Applications of Attachment Theory*. London: Routledge.

Bowlby, J. (1989). *Attachment and Loss, Volume 1: Attachment*. London: Penguin Books.

Bowlby, J. (1991). *Attachment and Loss, Volume 3: Loss*. London: Penguin Books.

Brave A., & Ferrid, H. (1990). John Bowlby and feminism. *Journal of the Institute For Self Analysis*, 4(1): 30–35.

Bremner, J. D. (2002). *Does Stress Damage the Brain?* New York: Norton.

Bretherton, I., & Waters, E. (Eds.) *Monographs of the Society for Research in Child Development*, 50: 66–104.

Burlingham, D., & Freud, A. (1942). *Young Children in Wartime*. London: Allen and Unwin.

Byng-Hall, J. (1991). The application of attachment theory to understanding and treatment in family therapy. In: C. M. Parkes, Stevenson-Hinde & Marris (Eds.), *Attachment Across the Life Cycle*. London: Routledge.

Christie, N. (1995). *The Crime Control as Industry: Towards Gulags, Western Style?* New York: Routledge.

Delgado, J. M. R. (1968). Recent advances in neurophysiology. In: *The Present Status of Psychotropic Drugs* (pp. 36–48). New York: Excerpta Medica International Congress, Series 180.

Dyer, C. (2002). Parents get away with "murder". *The Guardian*, 1 November.

Eastmond, M. (1997). *The Dilemmas of Exile. Chilean Refugees in the USA*. ACTA Universitatis Gothoburgensis: Gothenburg Studies in Social Anthropology.

Finkelhor, D. (1983), Common features of family abuse. In: D. Finkelhor, R. J. Gelles, G. T. Hotaling & M. Straus (Eds.), *The Dark Side of Families* (pp. 17–28). London: Sage.

Fletcher, J. (1999). *Disappearing Acts: Gender, Power, and Relational Practice at Work.* Cambridge, MA: MIT Press.

Fonagy, P., & Target, M. (1997). Attachment and reflective function: their role in self organization. *Development and Psychopathology, 9:* 679–700.

Fonagy, P., Steele, M., Steele, H., & Target, M. (1997). *Reflective Functioning Manual, Version 4.1.* London: Psychoanalysis Unit, University College.

Fonagy, P., Steele, M., Steele, H., Leigh, T., Kennedy, R., Mattoon, G., & Target, M. (1995) Attachment, the reflective self and borderline states: the predictive specificity of the Adult Attachment Interview and pathological emotional development. In: S. Goldberg, R. Muir & J. Kerr (Eds.), *Attachment Theory, Social Developmental and Clinical Perspectives.* Hillsdale, NJ & London: The Analytic Press.

Friedan, B. (1994). *The Fountain of Age.* London: Vintage Press.

Gelles, R. J. (1978). Violence towards children in the United States. *American Journal of Orthopsychiatry, 48:* 580–592.

Gilligan, J. (1996). *Violence, Our Deadly Epidemic and Its Causes.* New York: Grosset Putnam.

Gilligan, J. (2001). *Preventing Violence.* London: Thames and Hudson.

Greer, G. (1999). *The Whole Woman.* London: Doubleday.

Grossman, K. (1985). Maternal sensitivity and the newborn's orientation responses as related to quality of attachment in northern Germany. In: I. Bretherton & E. Waters (Eds.), *Growing Points of Attachment Theory and Research* (pp. 233–256). *Monographs of the Society for Research in Child Development, 50*(1–2): 209.

Guardian Weekly (2002). Comment and analysis. 31 January–6 February.

Hagan, J. (1994). *Crime and Disrepute.* London: Pine Forge Press.

Halperin, D. S., Bouvier, P., Jaffe, P. D., Mounoud, R. L., Pawlak, C. H., Laederach, J., Wicky, H. R., & Astie, F. (1996). The prevalence of child sexual abuse among adolescents in Geneva: Results of a cross section survey. *British Medical Journal, 298:* 727–730.

Harlow, H. F., & Zimmerman, R. (1959). Affectionate responses in the infant monkey. *Science, 130:* 421.

Hartling, L., & Sparks, E. (2002). *Relational-cultural Practice: Working in a Nonrelational World: Work in Progress No 97.* Wellesley, MA, Working Paper Series.

Herman, J. (1992). *Trauma and Recovery: The Aftermath of Violence from Domestic Abuse to Political Terror*. New York: Basic Books.

Hesse, E. (1999). The adult Attachment Interview: historical and current perspectives, In: J. Cassidy & P. R. Shaver (Eds.), *Handbook of Attachment* (pp. 395–433). New York: Guilford Press.

Hesse, E., Main, M., Yost-Abrams, K., & Rifkin, A. (2003). Unresolved states regarding loss or abuse have "second generation" effects: Disorganization, role-inversion, and frightening ideation in the off-spring of traumatized, non-maltreated parents. In: M. Solomon & D. J. Siegel (Eds.), *Healing Trauma*. New York: Norton.

Iacoboni, M., Woods, R. P., Brass, M., Bekkering, H., Mazziotta, J. C., & Rizzolatti, G. (1999). Cortical mechanisms of human imitation. *Science, 286*: 2526–2528.

Johnson, S. M. (1996). *Creating Connection: The Practice of Emotionally Focused Marital Therapy*. New York: Brunner/Mazel.

Johnson, S. M. (2002). *Emotionally Focused Couple Therapy with Trauma Survivors: Strengthening Attachment Bonds*. New York/London: The Guilford Press.

Johnson, S. M., & Lebow, J. (2000). The "coming of age" of couple therapy: a decade review. *Journal of Marital and Family Therapy, 26*: 1.

Jordan, J. (1999). *Toward Connection and Competence: Work in Progress No 83*. Wellesley MA, Working Paper Series.

Kaminer, W. (1995). *Its All the Rage: Crime and Culture*. New York: Addison Wesley.

Kandel, E. R. (1998). A new intellectual framework for psychiatry. *American Journal of Psychiatry, 155*: 457–469.

Kohler, A., & Alcock, N. (1976). An empirical table of structural violence. *Journal of Peace Research, 13*: 343–356.

Le Doux, J. (2002). *The Synaptic Self*. New York: Viking Press.

Lees, S. (1997). *Ruling Passions, Sexual Violence, Reputation and the Law*. Buckingham: Open University Press.

Lorenz, K. Z. (1957) [1935]. *Der Kumpen in der Unmelt des Vogels*. In: C. H. Schille (Ed. & Trans.), *Instinctive Behaviour*. New York: International University Press.

Macdonald, B., & Rich, C. (1984). *Look Me in the Eye: Old Women Ageing and Ageism*. San Francisco: Spinster's Ink.

Main, M. (1991). Metacognitive knowledge, metacognitive monitoring, and singular (coherent) vs. multiple (incoherent) model of attachment: findings and directions for future research. In: C. M. Parkes,

J. Stevenson-Hinde & P. Marris (Eds.), *Attachment Across the Life Cycle* (pp. 127–159). London: Routledge.

Main, M. (1994). *A move to the level of representation in the study of attachment organization: implications for psychoanalysis.* Annual Research Lecture to the British Psycho-Analytic Society: London, July 1994.

Main, M., & Cassidy, J. (1988). Categories of response to reunion with parent at age 6: predictable from infant attachment classifications and stable over a 1 month period. *Developmental Psychology*, 24: 1–12.

Main, M., & Hesse, E. (1990). Parents' unresolved traumatic experiences are related to infant disorganized attachment status: is frightening behaviour the linking mechanism? In: M. T. Greenberg, D. Cicchetti & E. M. Cummings (Eds.), *Attachment in the Pre-school Years* (pp. 161–182). Chicago: The University of Chicago Press.

Main, M., & Hesse, E. (1992). Disorganized/disorientated infant behaviour in the Strange Situation, lapses in monitoring of reasoning and discourse during the parent's Adult Attachment Interview, and Dissociative States. In: M. Ammanati & D. Stern (Eds), *Attachment and Psychoanalysis* (pp. 21–56). Rome: Gius Laterga e Figli.

Main, M., Kaplan, K., & Cassidy, J. (1985). Security in infancy, childhood and adulthood. A move to the level of representation. In: *Growing Points of Attachment Theory and Research.*

Main, M., Kaplan, K., & Cassidy, J. (1985). Security in infancy, childhood and adulthood: a move to the level of representation. In: I. Bretherton & E. Waters (Eds.), *Monographs of the Society for Research in Child Development*, 50: 66–104.

Malamuth, M. (1981). Rape proclivity among men. *Journal of Social Issues*, 37: 4.

Masters, W. H., & Johnson, V. E. (1970). *Human Sexual Inadequacy.* London: J&A Churchill.

McAlister, A., Sandstrom, P., Puska, P., Veijo, A., Chereches, R., & Heidmets L.-T. (2001). Attitudes towards war, killing, and punishment of children among young people in Estonia, Finland, Romania, the Russian Federation, and the USA. *Bulletin of the World Health Organization*, 79: 382–387.

McCarney, W. (1996). Domestic violence. *British Juvenile and Family Courts Society Newsletter*, April: 1–3.

Mead, G. H. (1934). *Mind, Self and Society From the Standpoint of a Social Behaviorist.* Chicago, London: Chicago University Press.

Meadow, R. (1989). Epidemiology of child abuse. *British Medical Journal*, 298: 727–730.

Meaney, M. J. (2001). Maternal care, gene expression, and the transmission of individual differences in stress reactivity across the generations. *Annual Review of Neuroscience*, 24: 1161–1192.

Milad, M. R., & Quirk, G. J. (2002). Neurones in medial prefrontal cortex signal memory for fear extinction. *Nature*, 420(4): 114–142.

Milgram, S. (1974). *Obedience to Authority, an Experimental View*. London: Harper Row.

Miller, A. (1989). *Thou Shalt Not Be Aware: Society's Betrayal of the Child*. London: Pluto Press.

Miller, A. (1991). *Banished Knowledge*. London: Virago.

Miller, A. (2001). *For Your Own Good: The Roots of Violence in Child-rearing*. London: Virago.

Miller, J. (1996). *Search and Destroy: African American Males in the Criminal Justice System*. New York: Cambridge University Press.

NSPCC (1966). *Childhood Matters*. The Report of the National Commission of Inquiry into the Prevention of Child Abuse, The Stationery Office.

Orbach, S. (1994). *What's Really Going On Here?* London: Virago.

Parkes, C. M. (1964). The effects of bereavement on physical and mental health. *British Medical Journal*, 2: 274–279.

Phillips, A. (1988). *Winnicott*. London: Fontana.

Rauch, S. L., van der Kolk, B. A., Fisler, R. E., Alprt, N. M., Orr, S. P., Savage, C. R., Fischman, A. J., Jenike, M. A., & Pitman, R. K. (1996). A symptom provocation study of post traumatic stress disorder using positron emission tomography and script driven imagery. *Archives of General Psychiatry*, 53: 380–387.

Richman, N. (1998). *In the Midst of the Whirlwind: A Manual for Helping Refugee Children*. Stoke on Trent: Trentham Books.

Robertson, J. (1952). *A Two-Year-Old Goes to Hospital* (film). London: Tavistock.

Russell, D. (1993). *Philadelphia Daily News*, 3. 5 October.

Sabini, J., & Silver, M. (1982). *Moralities of Daily Life*. Oxford: Oxford University Press.

Schore, A. N. (1994). *Affect Regulation and the Origin of the Self: The Neurobiology of Emotional Development*. Hillsdale, NJ: Erlbaum.

Schore, A. N. (1996). Experience dependent maturation of a regulatory system in the orbital pre-frontal cortex and the origin of developmental psychopathology. *Development and Psychopathology*, 8: 59–87.

Schore, A. N. (2003). *Affect Dysregulation and the Damage to the Self.* New York: Norton.

Siegel, D. J. (1999). *The Developing Mind: How Relationships and the Brain Interact to Shape Who We Are.* New York: Guilford.

Siegel, D. J. (2001). Toward an interpersonal neurobiology of the developing mind: attachment relationships, "mindsight" and neural integration. *Infant Mental Health Journal*, 22(1–2): 67–94.

Siegel, D. J., & Hartzell, M. (2003). *Parenting from the Inside Out: How a Deeper Self-understanding Can Help You Raise Children Who Thrive.* New York: Penguin Putnam.

Southgate, J. (1990). Towards a dictionary of advocate based self analysis. *Journal of the Institute for Self-Analysis*, 4: 1.

Spitz, R. E. (1945). *Hospitalism: An Enquiry into the Genesis of Psychiatric Conditions in Early Childhood.* Reprinted from *The Journal of The Psycho-Analytic Study of the Child*, Volume 1.

Stoller, R. J. (1975). *Perversion, the Erotic Form of Hatred.* London: Karnac.

Straus, M. B. (1991). Discipline and deviance: physical punishment of children and violence and other crime in adulthood. *Social Problems*, 38: 133–154.

Suomi, S. (2003). How gene-environment interactions can shape the development of socioemotional regulation in rhesus monkeys. In: B. S. Zuckerman & A. F. Lieberman (Eds.), *Socioemotional Regulation: Dimensions, Developmental Trends, and Influences.* Skillman, NJ: Johnson and Johnson.

Teicher, M. (2002). The neurobiology of child abuse. *Scientific American*, March: 68–75.

Troy, M., & Sroufe, L. A. (1987). Victimisation among preschoolers: role of attachment relationship history. *Journal of American Academy of Child and Adolescent Psychiatry*, 26: 166–172.

van der Kolk, B. A. (1989). The compulsion to repeat the trauma: re-enactment, re-victimisation and masochism. *Psychiatric Clinics of North America*, 12: 389–411.

van der Kolk, B. A. (1996). The body keeps the score: approaches to the psychobiology of post traumatic stress disorder. In: B. A. van der Kolk, A. C. McFarlane, & L. Weisaeth (Eds.), *Traumatic Stress: the Effects of Overwhelming Experience on Mind, Body, and Society* (pp. 214–241). New York: Guildford Press.

van der Kolk, B. A., van der Hart, O., & Marmar, C. R (1996). Dissociation and information processing in posttraumatic stress disorder. In: B. A. van der Kolk, McFarlane, & Weisaeth (Eds.), *Traumatic Stress* (pp. 303–327). New York/London: Guilford Press.

Watt, G. C. M. (1996). All together now: why social deprivation matters to everyone. *British Medical Journal, 312*: 1026–1029.

Wheeler, M. A., Stuss, D. T., & Tulving, E. (1997). Toward a theory of episodic memory: the frontal lobes and autonoetic consciousness. *Psychological Bulletin, 121*: 331–354.

Wolfgang, P. (1958). *Patterns in Criminal Homicide*. New York: John Wiley and Sons.

Woodcock, J. (2000). Refugee children and families: theoretical and clinical approaches. In: K. Dwivedi (Ed.), *Helping Children and Adolescents with Post Traumatic Stress Disorder* (pp. 213–239). London: Whurr.

Zulueta, de F. (1993). *From Pain to Violence, the Roots of Human Destructiveness*. London: Whurr.

U.W.E.L. LEARNING RESOURCES